Artists' **Modernist Houses**

Artists' **Modernist Houses**

Harriet Thorpe

BATSFORD

Contents

Introduction

'Buildings do not merely provide physical shelter or facilitate distinct activities. In addition to housing our fragile bodies and actions, they also need to house our minds, memories, desires, and dreams. Our buildings are crucial extensions of ourselves, both individually and collectively.'

Juhani Pallasmaa, '*Towards a Neuroscience of Architecture*' (1)

We can read a lot about a person through their home. According to Finnish architect Juhani Pallasmaa, our living spaces are externalised reflections of who we are inside. Artists are a fascinating group to examine this theory: thoughtful, radical, brave and expressive individuals, who often pre-empt change and exist outside imposed societal binaries.

In addition to the artworks themselves, artists' houses offer alternative insights into their personal lives, and the conditions behind that creation. While an artwork expresses an image or concept, houses express the structure of a lifestyle – joining the two is like connecting the psychological and the physical.

When we are moved by an artwork, we are curious about how and where it was created, and houses are an excellent place to start. Rather than just reading a book and using one's imagination, they offer multiple sensory dimensions to experience this. Many of these artists are so committed to their creation that they can't help but live inside a total and all-consuming extension of it.

Bernat Klein's house and studio (see entry 26) in Scotland was like a living, dimensional portfolio where colour, nature, abstraction, textiles and design met in pure concord; his careful upkeep of its vision reflected the same ambition and discipline that he applied to his work. Shelley Klein, his daughter, writes about her personal experience of living in the house in her book *The See-Through House*: 'It was almost impossible – to my mind, at least – to separate the two things from each other. My father was the house. The house was my father.' (2)

OPPOSITE
Bernat Klein with his family at their Scotland home, built in 1958.

Living spaces are closely connected to our identity: reflecting both who we are and, to some extent, who we aspire to be.

Living spaces are closely connected to our identity: reflecting both who we are and, to some extent, who we aspire to be. They are shaped by the requirements of our identity, yet we can also shape them into whatever we like, moulding our habits around them and perhaps slowly transforming to embody the values they define. The Modern Age was a time of reinvention and optimism – reactive approaches and the accelerating exchange of progressive ideas inspired people to boldly break with the inherited past and start fresh. So, if designing a house is akin to designing a lifestyle – in examining the meeting of Modern art and Modern architecture, the conscious act of design according to an artistic movement or style is an act of translating it into the dimensions of life.

Theo van Doesburg (see entry 4) believed that the environment in which art was created was vital to the resulting expression. For him, the best artwork was one that did not reveal the impression of the human hand: his works echo the language of the machine, geometric, precise and perfect. Consequently, he wrote how a studio could help to achieve this: 'This perfection depends on everything surrounding it, absolute lucidity, stable light, a bright atmosphere. [...] The artist's studio will be like a bell jar or a hollow crystal.' (3)

There are many house-studios in this book, yet some examples are just houses and a few are apartments, studios and hybrid forms that show clear Modernist design interventions and approaches. Some artists commissioned an architect: they believed in the vision of the architect to interpret their way of life and gave them carte blanche to do so. Others collaborated with an architect, mixing ideas and influences. Some artists used the

OPPOSITE
Ruth Asawa and her children around the kitchen table at their home in San Francisco in the mid-1960s.

SALT

form of architecture as living sculpture, and other artists took on the formal role of architect themselves.

Amaza Lee Meredith (see entry 37) did the latter against all odds: a Black woman living in 1930s post-segregation Lynchburg, Virginia, who was prohibited from studying architecture, yet designed and built a Modern house for herself and her female Black life partner – all while working as an art educator and inspiring others to become artists. She broke with nearly all imposed past conventions and carved out her own utopia aligned with her way of life.

In the early 20th century, Modern art and Modern architecture formed a reciprocal relationship for some time: united in the goal to aesthetically and functionally improve society. Yet this happened at a time of huge social and political change, against a backdrop of two world wars, the Civil Rights Movement, feminism, the gay rights movement and post-colonial independence movements. Modern art and Modern architecture were galvanised and shaped by all of these although the disciplines did not necessarily progress in such unison.

The artists' houses that are curated here are not representative of a history of the 20th century, yet their stories contribute to learning about lives lived in the Modern Age – which are threaded together in various ways in the essays in this book. After all, their very existence in this selection relies on and is limited by access to photography, preservation, letters, books, archives, memories, foundations and estates.

This leaves us at the peril of dominant Western-centric histories of Modern art and architecture that exist as a result of centuries of imperialism and colonialism that positioned Western

While art can move you in all kinds of directions, the domestic realm feels deeply sensory and grounding.

perspectives dominantly in academic study and knowledge production. Here, there are a lack of Modern artist's Modern houses located in Asia, the Middle East and Africa that exist in many forms. The examples presented largely follow a Western 'canon', though we have tried to expand this.

In the curation, the artist and architect are singled out as the creators of these houses to construct a comparative framework, yet creation is never singular. There are always many other artists involved – from partners, to families, patrons and mentors – whose artistry might exist in other skills. For example, it was the partner of Gordon Onslow Ford (see entry 45), Jacqueline – a writer, who had previously commissioned her own house from leading Modern architect Richard Neutra in Los Angeles – who played the important role of mediator between artist and architect during their collaboration – 'often suggesting a picnic somewhere on the beautiful site to break an impasse'. (4) Sometimes creativity is all about those picnics – and the people who suggest them, who might not always go down in history.

When I visit an artist's house, I always find it a joyful and a reflective process. It's freeing somehow to feel immersed in the world of someone you admire – someone who created a work of art that so powerfully expressed an experience and moment in time that it went down in history; it feels restful, sacred and cinematic. While art can move you in all kinds of directions, the domestic realm feels deeply sensory and grounding: human, personal and tangible. Somehow being in an artist's house makes me feel self-reflective too as their externalised thoughts inspire me to look deeper into my own internalised ones and wonder how they emerge in life.

01

André Wogenscky and Marta Pan

Saint-Rémy-lès-Chevreuse, Île-de-France, France

Logic and emotion, function and poetry, curves and lines – all find harmony at the house and studio of this architect-artist couple.

South-west of Paris in the leafy suburb of Saint-Rémy-lès-Chevreuse lies the dynamic house-studio of Hungarian-French sculptor Marta Pan (1923–2008) and French architect André Wogenscky (1916–2004). Built 1950–52, the design was a collaboration between the artist and architect couple – Wogenscky, an expert of Modernist function, and Pan, a protagonist of organic balance.

Leaning into the sloping landscape, the house is a box, sculpted with a series of carved and extruded shapes, first appearing abstract, and then functional, each working together to achieve an asymmetric balance of heaviness and lightness. The front is punctuated by a red-painted section inside a large protruding rectangular concrete frame. Other facades feature smaller black concrete frames; at the back, a recessed void opens up a covered terrace. The rooftop solarium is another 'facade', intersected by a curved windbreak.

The young couple, who married in 1952, would live in this house together their whole lives. Pan had moved to Paris in 1947 after studying at the Budapest Academy of Arts. On arrival, her organic, abstract sculptures made of materials such as wood, bronze, marble and Plexiglas attracted the attention of esteemed sculptor Constantin Brancusi. She met Wogenscky, who had studied architecture at the Académie des Beaux-Arts in Paris, at the offices of leading Modernist architect Le Corbusier, where he worked from 1936 as an important contributor.

The interior plan of the house is based upon the 'Modulor' measurement, developed by Wogenscky and Le Corbusier and based on human proportions. On the ground floor, interiors flow without walled divisions, guided instead by varying ceiling heights and elements such as the suspended metal fireplace and a sunken conversation pit.

Pan's workshop was on this level, connected to the garden that inspired her, while Wogenscky's studio was on the upper floor, with a slim horizontal window as, for him, nature was a distraction. Vibrant details include the bright red sculpted wooden handles, a boiler with colourful piping and Pan's sculptures that capture the

OPPOSITE
The sculptural exterior of the house.

Interiors flow without walled divisions, guided instead by varying ceiling heights and elements such as the suspended metal fireplace and a sunken conversation pit.

tension and balance of bodies in space.

This house was the couple's first architectural collaboration of many. Wogenscky established his own architecture studio in 1956. Pan contributed sculptural works to his public buildings – further developing the relationship between art and architecture, edges and curves, function and humanity – on a larger scale from Beirut to Japan.

An expression of their shared life and work, the house was added to the list of France's historical monuments in 1997 and became the Marta Pan – André Wogenscky Foundation in 2011, which is open to the public to visit.

ABOVE
The ground floor interior.

02

Sophie Taeuber-Arp and Jean Arp

Clamart, Île-de-France, France

Geometric textile designs scaled up into the architectural plans for a house, where this artist couple lived together and hosted friends.

From 1928, Swiss artist Sophie Taeuber (1889–1943) designed a house and studio for herself and her partner French artist Jean Arp (also known as Hans Arp, 1886–1966). Located south-west of Paris in Clamart, on the edge of the Meudon Forest, it was a creative haven for the couple and their artistic friends such as Sonia and Robert Delaunay, André Breton, Alexander Calder, Max Ernst and Marcel Duchamp – that was, until the Nazi occupation of Paris drove them away in 1940 during World War II.

A true Modernist, Taeuber was a multidextrous artist with a limitless imagination, who transformed her ideas across mediums with ease, eventually scaling up to architecture with this house. Born in Switzerland, she studied applied arts in Munich, then became a teacher of textile design in Zurich. There, she developed her geometric patterns into Neo-plastic abstract compositions, freely expanding her output to painting, sculpture, costume, stage design and dance.

It was also in Zurich, in 1915, where she met Arp. He co-founded the Dada movement in 1916 with the 'Cabaret Voltaire' alongside fellow artists who had fled World War I to neutral Switzerland. The movement subverted the absurdity of war through radical spontaneity and performative protest. Taeuber and Arp began to work collaboratively and joined 'Das Neue Leben', a group that proposed the integration of abstract art and everyday life.

They married in 1922 (Sophie became 'Taeuber-Arp') and moved to Strasbourg. There she designed a series of interiors, notably the Café de l'Aubette, an abstract Gesamtkunstwerk inside a Neoclassical 18th-century building, created in collaboration with Jean Arp and Theo van Doesburg, the Dutch founder of De Stijl (see entry 4).

It was with all of this experience that she designed the house built between 1927 and 1929, which is informed by Bauhaus principles: a simple rectangular cube over three floors, built with rough local burrstone, contrasted with cast concrete entrances and balconies. Living spaces are on the ground floor; upstairs, on

OPPOSITE
The stone and concrete house.

Arp developed his sculptural language of honed organic forms and the couple hosted lively lunches with artists from Paris.

the first floor, is Arp's studio, then at the top Taeuber-Arp's studio with a big window overlooking the garden. A colourful (blue, yellow and grey) and modular wooden furniture system of stackable elements adapt into bookcases, coffee tables and desks.

There Arp developed his sculptural language of smooth and honed organic forms and the couple hosted lively lunches with artists from Paris. In her letters, Taeuber-Arp grappled with balancing domestic and work life under one roof: expected to be a host, as housewives of the period were, while commanding the respect for her ideas to be heard equally at the table.

After the couple left Paris to flee the Nazis, Taeuber-Arp would never return to the house because she died in 1943 from accidental carbon-monoxide poisoning in Switzerland. Arp's second wife, Marguerite Arp-Hagenbach, established the Fondation Arp in 1978 at the house, dedicated to the cultural heritage of Jean Arp and Sophie Taeuber-Arp.

OPPOSITE
The interior of the house; now a gallery displaying work by Jean Arp.

03 André Bloc | Claude Parent

Meudon, Île-de-France, France

A house, studio and laboratory for ideas – where imagination came to life in its most total way through expressive 'living sculptures' in the garden.

André Bloc (1896–1966) fused sculpture, architecture and living in a series of houses and studios he designed across his lifetime, which became his laboratories for creativity and thinking. Here in Meudon outside of Paris, his Modernist home and studio was flanked by two experimental *sculptures habitacles* – or 'living sculptures' – which captured his radical approach that crossed disciplines and theories.

Born in Algiers, Bloc's family emigrated to France in 1898. He studied as an engineer, then in the 1920s, inspired by meetings

BELOW
One of Bloc's 'living sculptures': a softly Cubist cave.

OVERLEAF
The Villa Bloc.

Bloc described his experimental *sculptures habitacles* as 'functional abstraction'.

with architects Auguste Perret and Le Corbusier, began to study architecture – all the while developing a career in magazine publishing. From the 1940s, he then moved into sculpture. In 1951, he co-founded the avant-garde 'Groupe Espace' with Félix Del Marle. The group drew connections between art and social impact in architectural and urban environments.

The Villa Bloc, designed in the early 1950s, is a Modernist design of local stone, brick, concrete and glass. Situated at the lowest point of the plot, it feels immersed in nature, with a curved plan that opens up to the garden with large floor-to-ceiling windows across the facade, partly designed in a rhythmic vertical grid. The open-plan living space has black stone floor tiles and a red staircase curving up to the first floor. Bloc designed furniture especially for this house, such as the sinuous 'Boomerang' desk with its curvy zig-zag legs.

A second building designed by French architect Claude Parent (1923–2016) was added to the plot in 1956: the 'guardian's house', the ground floor of which became Bloc's studio. It echoes the language of the main house with two cubes separated by a staircase. Bloc designed a colourful stained-glass window for the lower level.

The pair would go on to imagine other houses – on the Côte d'Azur and in the fishing village of Carboneras in Spain. Parent would eventually challenge the rules of Modernism with his concept of the Fonction Oblique, based on the sloping ramp, marking the advent of Deconstructivism.

From 1962 to 1966, Bloc added his *habitacles* to the garden, which he described as 'functional abstraction'. One is a softly Cubist cave of brick vaults, and the other a labyrinthine belvedere tower. Their eccentric characteristics attracted architects such as Oscar Niemeyer, as well as film directors William Klein and Jean-Luc Godard.

After Bloc's accidental death at the age of 70 in New Delhi, the future of the house was uncertain, yet it was classified as a historic monument in 1983 and then found a custodian in French gallerist Natalie Seroussi, who preserves and champions its legacy today.

04 Theo and Nelly van Doesburg

Meudon-Val-Fleury, Île-de-France, France

An incubator for artists of the 20th century and today, this house and studio was constructed from the rigorous geometry of the De Stijl movement.

The Modern art movement of De Stijl (1917–31) was established to define a universal visual language based upon the mathematical geometries of horizontal and vertical lines and shapes. Founded by a group of artists including Piet Mondrian and Theo van Doesburg (1883–1931) in the Netherlands, it emerged first as a magazine, which coined the term 'Neo-plastic' for the first time, before synthesizing its vision across disciplines as a precursor to the Bauhaus.

Perfectly encapsulated by Dutch architect Gerrit Rietveld's 'Rietveld Schröder House' of 1924 in Utrecht, De Stijl also came to architectural life at the house-studio of artists Theo and Nelly van Doesburg. The couple met in 1920 in The Hague and embarked on an adventure as a musical duo on the Dada scene – Nelly (aged 21 at the time they met) on the piano and Theo (then aged 37) singing. Nelly's inheritance allowed them to build a house in Meudon-Val-Fleury, a suburb of Paris – close to the home of the Arps (see entry 2), who they had met in Zurich and collaborated with on the interiors of L'Aubette in Strasbourg.

Van Doesburg had been developing the idea of 'visual architecture' with Dutch architect Cornelis van Eesteren. A model of their 'Maison d'Artiste' was shown in the first De Stijl exhibition of 1923, to highlight how form and colour could create spatial dynamism. This house that Theo designed with architect Abraham Elzas was a realistic adaptation of these ideas, formed of two interlocking white cubes, one for the double-height studio and the other for the residence.

OPPOSITE
The front facade of the house.

The house is formed of two interlocking white cubes, one for the double-height artist's studio and the other for the residence.

A spiral staircase circulates up to the roof terrace; while a Mondrian-style stained-glass roof-light illuminates the library.

On the front facade, a square wall hides a diagonal staircase that leads to the blue first-floor entrance door sheltered by a concrete canopy. There are four horizontal windows and two further doors (in yellow and red). The rear facade features the large double-height window of the studio, through which a spiral staircase circulates up to the roof terrace, and below the studio cube a covered terrace is connected to the ground-floor kitchen.

Inside, there's a Mondrian-style stained-glass roof-light illuminating the library; a scheme of fixed grey concrete tables in the studio, kitchen and music room, originally painted with yellow tops; patterned tiled floors of white, grey, black, yellow and red in the bathroom, kitchen and library; pale grey walls in the studio; and a dark grey balustrade.

Just one year after the house was finished, in 1931, Theo died of a heart attack. Nelly lived on in the Meudon house for the rest of her life. She became a friend and advisor to American art collector Peggy Guggenheim, travelling to the US during the war to promote Theo's work. When she died in 1975, the studio-house and its collection were inherited by Wies van Moorsel, Nelly's niece, who implemented her plan to donate it to the nation (it gained protected status in 1981) and open it for artists' residencies.

ABOVE
The double-height artist's studio.

05

Fernand Léger

Lisores, Normandy, France

A Modernist mosaic on the gable wall of a vernacular farmhouse captures the tension between the past and future in the early 20th century.

In a secluded valley of meadows and a winding river, in the municipality of Lisores in Normandy, the old rural farmhouse of Fernand Léger (1881–1995) has been transformed into a modern work of art with a luminous mosaic mural of a farmer and a cow on its gable wall. The dynamic lines, colour blocks and simplified forms of the artwork create an almost provocative contrast to the traditional, whitewashed vernacular architecture of the building, representing a tension between two concurrent ways of life in the early Modern period.

The farmhouse was a place where Léger retreated throughout his life to grapple with the intensity of modern 20th-century life. He inherited it from his mother in 1922 and, far from being a 'Modernist' house, it had no running water or telephone. It was an antidote to Modernism, where he lived as an 'avant-garde peasant', painting in his studio, collecting flints and leaves, and often inviting friends from Paris such as Constantin Brancusi, Le Corbusier and Charlotte Perriand to gather and cook around the large hearth.

After his rural upbringing, Léger had apprenticed with an architect, before taking up art. He was conscripted into the French Army in 1914, resorting to drawing on ammunition boxes and military maps. The experience expanded his social consciousness, and his work developed with the emergence of strong, contrasting lines and bold colours, often outlining urban and machine-led motifs.

In between travels to New York in the 1930s, he collaborated with architects and interior designers including Buckminster Fuller, Robert Mallet-Stevens and Charlotte Perriand – imaging his artwork with new dimensionality and further exploring the connection between painting and architecture. When he then became a refugee from World War II in America, his bold, graphic works positioned him as a forerunner to Pop Art. On his return to France, contrasts were even more extreme, as was his *joie de vivre*, exploring topics from leisure to nature, with shapes of the landscape, farm machinery, animals, flowers and trees.

In February 1952, he married Nadia Khodossievitch. After his sudden death in 1955, Nadia became custodian of the farm and his recently purchased land in Biot in the south of France. She worked to bring his architectural visions of both places to life: the Fernand Léger National Museum opened in Biot in 1960, with a modern design and huge abstract mosaic mural. After a series of updates, the Farm-Museum was inaugurated the same year: the distillery/bread oven was transformed into a chapel with stained-glass windows to a design by Léger himself and the mosaic was born in celebration of his legacy.

ABOVE
'The Farmer and the Cow' mosaic (1960), based on a painting by the artist.

ABOVE
The white facade
and statue of
Georges Pompidou.

06

Philolaos Tloupas

Saint-Rémy-lès-Chevreuse, Île-de-France, France

Layered into the landscape, this house emerged from the imagination of a sculptor, who took a hands-on approach to crafting its total design.

In the picturesque Chevreuse Valley near Paris, a steel statue of Georges Pompidou reaching a height of 4.5m (15ft) guards the entrance to this layered house-studio, designed by Greek artist Philolaos Tloupas (1923–2010), also known as just Philolaos. Pompidou, President of France from 1969 until his death in 1974, supported Modernism as a positive tool for society, and therefore was an apt guardian for this Modernist house.

Born in Greece, Philolaos studied at the Athens School of Fine Arts, and moved to Paris in the 1950s to continue his studies and develop his sculptural practice, which fused elements of Brutalism, Cubism and Arte Povera. He used raw natural and industrial materials such as wood, stone, concrete and stainless steel. His public commissions reached monumental scales, often in collaboration with architects – such as his Valence water towers with architect André Gomis (1971), or the imposing L'oiseau Mécanique (1972) in La Défense in Paris.

He first visited the area while teaching pottery and sculpture at the Ateliers éducatifs de Claireau between 1947 and 1967. It was in the 1960s that he decided to build his family home and studio there, beside a small forest in Saint-Rémy-lès-Chevreuse – not far from André Wogenscky and Marta Pan (see entry 1). He had grown up in a family of makers, with a self-sufficient, practical approach to living, and had already designed and built a family home with his father, a carpenter, in Greece. He began work on this new house in 1964, recording the construction process in a notebook.

Built into the natural slope of the land, the house has a functional layout where the domestic and workspace areas are separate, yet layered and visually connected to form a fluid way of life. A living space occupies a mezzanine overlooking the double-height studio, lit from skylights above like an industrial space, while the domestic rooms are more intimate in scale and have large windows with views to nature.

Architecture and interiors are united in a total scheme, with wall niches for sculptures, a moulded concrete bench and sculptural fireplace. Philolaos also designed custom furniture such as a wooden rocking chair, steel coffee table, a fruit bowl of stone pebbles, even cutlery and salt and pepper shakers – exemplifying his wide-reaching approach to art and design. After his death in 2010, his family preserved the house and studio as a work of art in itself, and an enduring manifesto of his life and work.

OPPOSITE
The artist's studio.

07

Amédée Ozenfant | Le Corbusier

Paris, France

The Early Modern house and studio represents the formative, collaborative relationship between artist and architect.

The house of French painter and writer Amédée Ozenfant (1886–1966) occupies a corner plot in the 14th arrondissement of Paris. As Le Corbusier's first built house, constructed between 1922 and 1924, it embodies the principles of his early architectural theories – with a concrete structure and grids of windows, more evocative of an industrial building rather than a domestic one.

The interior plan was attuned to Ozenfant's needs. The double-height studio on the second floor is illuminated to the maximum with daylight from its huge corner windows and zig-zag sawtooth roof-light. Two mezzanine levels create further space for a library and storage, while maintaining a dynamic sense of volume. The lower levels are reserved for living, with the main residence on the first floor, and a housekeeper's residence and garage on the ground floor.

Ozenfant was an early influence on Le Corbusier, who, when they met, was known as Charles-Edouard Jeanneret (1887–1965). The artist had moved to Paris in 1907 to continue his education in architecture and painting, and during World War I he began publishing the journal *L'Elan*, which sought to protect the avant-garde cultural spirit during wartime, placing him in contact with leading artists such as André Derain, Henri Matisse and Pablo Picasso to name a few.

After the war, Ozenfant and Le Corbusier met and bonded in their shared belief that Cubism had lost its edge. Together they founded the Purist art movement in 1918 to re-establish a more minimal, flat style of fragmented and two-dimensional shapes in neutral, muted colour schemes (opposite to the bright contrasting colours of De Stijl). The aesthetic responded to the language of technology and machines, with precision, clarity and economy, positioning itself as a new Classicism.

In many ways, Purist art echoed the flatness of an architectural plan, and in turn it influenced Le Corbusier's early Purist architecture. It was in the pages of their journal *L'Esprit Nouveau*, published between 1920 and 1925, that Le Corbusier penned the theories of his influential text *Vers une architecture* (commonly translated as *Towards a new architecture*) (1923), outlining

RIGHT
The exterior of the house and studio.

architectural rules of function and geometry that departed from Art Deco and formed the backbone of the Modern movement.

Le Corbusier's prototype dwelling, 'Pavillon de l'Esprit Nouveau', captured these Purist ideas on a global stage for the 1925 International Exposition of Decorative and Industrial Arts in Paris. After this, however, the relationship between Ozenfant and Le Corbusier ended. The artist established a painting school, the Académie Ozenfant, in his own studio in 1932. He travelled to London and New York in the 1930s, then, shortly before World War II, sold the house and eventually settled in Cannes. The Ozenfant house has since undergone several transformations, though the facades and roofs were protected in 1975.

10

08

Tamara de Lempicka, Jan and Joël Martel | Robert Mallet-Stevens

Paris, France

Art Deco met Bauhaus style at the 1920s apartment of a painter and house of two sculptors designed by architect Robert Mallet-Stevens.

Artist Tamara de Lempicka (1894–1980) hosted glamorous parties at her Paris apartment and studio, located within a building designed by French architect Robert Mallet-Stevens (1886–1945). It was a sleek setting for displaying her paintings – complete with a wood-panelled cocktail bar and shiny tubular steel furniture designed by her sister, Adrienne Gorska, one of the first qualified female architects in Europe.

Though her birthdate and place hold some ambiguity, it is generally agreed that de Lempicka was born in 1894 to Polish parents and grew up in Warsaw. She met her husband in St Petersburg and shortly after the Russian Revolution of 1917 left for Paris with her daughter. On arrival she began to study painting, inspired by the Old Masters and mentored by Cubist painter and art critic André Lhote.

At first, she signed her early paintings ' T. Lempitzky' (the male version of her last name), yet soon became a celebrated and liberated feminist icon – exhibiting at the Salon des Femmes Artistes Modernes in the 1930s. Her style encapsulated the free-flowing atmosphere of the interwar period and the energy of the Jazz Age, combining the lines of Art Deco and the dynamism of Futurism and Constructivism, with sculptural volumes of Classical art and chiaroscuro lighting of the Renaissance.

In the late 1920s, she moved into her apartment in Mallet-Stevens' modern building on Rue Méchain in the 14th arrondissement. Its playfully stacked concrete volume is split into two parts, six and nine levels high, which are distributed around a central staircase and elevator tower. The twelve apartments and two duplex studios featured amenities from sliding windows to built-in bath-tubs, as well as Art Deco metalwork by Jean Prouvé, stained glass by Louis Barillet and lighting by André Salomon.

Beyond her black patinated metal and chrome double-door, a studio with a soaring ceiling height of 5.4m (18ft) was lit by a

OPPOSITE
The studio of Jan and Joël Martel.

gridded wall of windows. On the upper mezzanine wall, an interior stained-glass and mirrored window with a geometric Art Deco pattern was designed by Louis Barillet and a sculptural ceiling lamp by René Herbst and André Salomon hung from the ceiling.

Mallet-Stevens completed this apartment building shortly after the more expressive stepped volume of the Hôtel Martel (1927). Located in the 16th arrondissement, the two-family house included a shared studio for sculptors, brothers Jan and Joël Martel. The architect was popular on the art scene, also designing the 1920s Villa Noailles in the south of France for Surrealist art collectors Charles and Marie-Laure de Noailles.

In 1938, amid the growing political unrest in Europe, de Lempicka and her second husband, the Austrian-Hungarian Baron Raoul Kuffner de Dioszegh (both had Jewish heritage), left Paris for New York, remaining in the US after the war. Later in her life, in 1976, de Lempicka moved to Cuernavaca, Mexico, to a house named Tres Bambus. When she passed away, her artist friend Victor Contreras, together with her daughter Kizette Foxhall, scattered her ashes from a helicopter above the Popocatépetl volcano according to her wishes.

Both the apartment of de Lempicka and the Hôtel Martel are privately owned, yet both of these Mallet-Stevens masterpieces, which capture the artistic spirit of Paris in the 1920s, have been preserved and classified as historic monuments.

ABOVE
The residents' staircase at the Rue Méchain apartment building.

These two Mallet-Stevens masterpieces capture the artistic spirit of Paris in the 1920s.

09 Claudio Caffetto | Fausto Bontempi

Brescia, Lombardy, Italy

An expressive family home and anchor for the Brescian art scene that eclectically collages Modern architectural movements.

In the 1960s, Italian artist Claudio Caffetto (1942–2022) began to imagine a house with his wife Franca Manera and their family, where art and life were inseparable. In 1972, he commissioned architect and friend Fausto Bontempi (b. 1935) to bring his vision to life, in Brescia on the edge of the town of Calcinato.

Unique from every angle and outlook, the expressive suburban house caused a stir in the neighbourhood during its two-year construction. Like a three-dimensional collage, it samples volumes, geometry and materials across architectural movements from Modernism to Brutalism.

The interior is a theatre of oblique angles, with tactile layers of wood, stone and metal, and shifting connections of ramps and walkways. Shelves, niches, lighting and handrails are all integrated, and sequences of rooms are guided by angles, compression and expansion. At the top of the house, a glass roof illuminates the studio and gallery with daylight.

Bontempi trained under Modern Italian architect Carlo Scarpa, whose influence can be seen in the sculpturally exposed concrete and circular cut-outs in the wedge-shaped buttresses. The primary colour scheme was informed by the Bauhaus.

The whole building reflects artist Caffetto's total view of art, which was rooted in craft and community. It was at just 14 years old, after the loss of his mother, that he began working as a draughtsman in the studio of architect Bruno Fedrigolli. He took evening classes in drawing and sculpture at the Brescian Artists' Association, and later enrolled to study art in Parma. After designing jugs and plates for local craftspeople, at 19 years old he opened a pewter workshop in Brescia, which later became an export business across Europe.

Continuing this kind of collaboration throughout his life, the house became a vibrant meeting place for international artists such as Dadamaino, Franco Grignani, Miguel Berrocal and many others. These encounters inspired Caffetto's 'Edizioni d'Arte Caffetto', an organization dedicated to artistic metal editions in bronze, aluminium, copper and pewter.

ABOVE
The house and its verdant garden.

Today, his abstract paintings and figurative sculptures in bronze, marble, wood and terracotta can still be experienced in situ, preserved by his daughters Metilde and Giovanna Caffetto who celebrate and share the house with the public.

'The Empress' takes the form of a giant female sphinx, which the artist described as a 'protective mother'.

10

Niki de Saint Phalle

Garavicchio, Tuscany, Italy

As a radical commitment to her largest work of art, this Modern feminist artist made a home inside a monumental sculpture named The Empress.

French American artist and sculptor Niki de Saint Phalle (1930–2002) always wanted to live inside a sculpture. Her dream materialised inside 'The Empress', a monumental sculpture-house within her fantastical Tarot Garden in southern Tuscany. She lived there for seven years, totally immersed in her artistic project, which began in 1979 and continued until her death.

'The Empress' takes the form of a giant female sphinx – a 'protective mother' as de Saint Phalle described it – with underfloor heating. Her bedroom was inside one of its colourful protruding breasts. The living space was a mirrored cave, with a long table, integrated benches, circular windows and a chandelier by Swiss artist Jean Tinguely (1925–1991), a close collaborator on the Tarot Garden and her partner between 1971 and 1991. In 1988, she also built a New York-style loft space under 'The Moon', which she said freed her from the heavy psychological weight of living inside a womb-like space.

The early works of de Saint Phalle, a self-taught artist, included performances (one involved shooting balls of paint with a gun), abstract paintings and assemblages of found consumer objects. Many were connected to her activism around issues such as racism, AIDS and feminism. In the 1960s, she became the only female member of the New Realist group with the likes of Jasper Johns and Robert Rauschenberg, and created her first 'Nanas': expressive, abstracted figures of liberated women, whose bulbous and joyful aesthetic can be seen in the sculptures of the Tarot Garden.

The tarot cards had always offered de Saint Phalle a guide to understanding the problems of life and, influenced by Spanish architect Antoni Gaudí's organic mosaicked Parc Güell in Barcelona, she began designing ideas for a garden of monumental sculptures of the major arcana 'characters' of the tarot (the 22 named cards). Then, in 1978, acquaintances Marella, Carlo and Nicola Caracciolo offered her 14 acres of land in Tuscany and the freedom to build her vision.

OPPOSITE
The mirrored living space of The Empress.

In the undulating landscape, between olive trees, her colourful symbolic sculptures reach between 12 and 15 metres (40–50ft) in height. They were scaled up by eye from models into welded metal structures, which were clad in wire mesh and sprayed with gunite cement. Their colourful mosaics of ceramics, glass and mirror were directly crafted onto their surfaces, dimensionally modelled as tiny pyramids, snail-shell swirls, coral-like spikes and rational dots and cubes.

Here, 'Modernism' lies in her abstract style and feminist power, as well as in the organic process of building with modern materials, that could be compared to the freeform architecture of French architect Jacques Couëlle or Hungarian architect Antti Lovag in France. As well as a home, 'The Empress' became a site office, an artist's studio, and a meeting place for coffee breaks and dinners with the fluctuating construction team of artists, craftspeople and locals, including ceramicist Venera Finocchiaro, sculptor Pierre Marie Lejeune (who made integrated furniture and pathways) and architect Mario Botta (who designed the fortress-like entrance gate).

De Saint Phalle designed other monumental and architectural sculptures around the world, such as 'Queen Califia's Magical Circle' near San Diego, California, and a dragon-themed playhouse in Belgium. Yet the most immersive and largest is the Tarot Garden, which she created a foundation to manage and preserve in 1999; it remains open to the public to visit today.

OPPOSITE
A walkway leading into The Emperor, another sculpture in the Tarot Garden.

11

Giacomo Balla

Rome, Italy

Family life inside this Futurist apartment was filled with colour and pattern, capturing the electric magic of modern city life beyond.

Behind the door of this family apartment lies a colourful cosmos of patterned murals and crafted symbolism. Welcome to the home of Italian painter Giacomo Balla (1871–1958), his wife Elisa Marcucci, and their two daughters Luce and Elica. Instrumental in founding the early 20th-century Futurist movement, Balla translated the accelerating, electrifying energy of modernising society into his art and home interior.

The Balla family moved into the apartment in 1929, and together they dreamt up decorative schemes with matching furniture, wallpaper and tiling. Elisa made tablecloths, and the girls painted murals on the walls. The hallway became a vortex of green, yellow and blue motifs, with matching lampshades and coat-hooks. The kitchen was bedecked in painted flowers and birds, and Elica's bedroom with fluffy clouds.

Giacomo Balla was among a group of artists who interpreted the ideas of the poet and editor Filippo Tommaso Marinetti's 1909 political Futurist manifesto into art. Balla's work moved away from Futurism's political ideas of nationalist expansion, and towards finding an aesthetic language of the moment. His enraptured observation of the evolving everyday resulted in bold brushstrokes and modern motifs, combining ideas of Cubism and Divisionism. He conjured movement with sweeping and diagonal lines, capturing the wizardry of new technology – from street lights to photography.

Balla's art often expanded beyond the canvas: he designed clothes and toys, as well as murals for the interior of Bal Tic Tac, a Futurist cabaret club. In adventuring into multifarious dimensions, he was able to immersively capture the all-consuming intensity of living in the future.

Casa Balla became known locally as 'The Magician's House', and the family welcomed curious visitors every Sunday. Balla lived there until his death in 1958, and his daughters stayed until their deaths in the 1990s. The apartment was protected as cultural heritage in 2004, then underwent restoration by the MAXXI (National Museum of 21st Century Art in Rome). It continues to transport visitors back in time to when technology began to transform everyday life in European cities.

OPPOSITE
The artist's studio.

BALLA

12

Arnaldo Pomodoro, Giovanni Lana | Ettore Sottsass

Milan, Italy

Step inside the ingenious, integrated interiors of a Radical Italian architect who playfully compacted space and function for urban living.

In the late 1960s, sculptor Arnaldo Pomodoro (1926–2025) bought an unremarkable attic apartment in Milan to use as a studio-meets-pied-á-terre for entertaining patrons and friends. He commissioned Italian architect Ettore Sottsass (1917–2007) to transform it with a dynamic, dimensional scenography for working and living, integrating art, storage, technology and comfort.

Built in collaboration with young architect Bruno Scagliola and carpenter Giuseppe Baraldi, this performative platform subdivided the interior into functions. It starts as a staircase made of rosewood – embedded with cabinets, drawers and shelves – which leads up to a small bedroom. A library with a record player tucked beneath the staircase becomes a counterweight to a marble dining table. Chrome-plated perforated sheets and white plastic laminate panels frame windows and sliding layers of frosted glass.

Artist Pomodoro began his career working as a surveyor, before turning to sculpture in the 1950s. He relocated to Milan, meeting influential artists such as Lucio Fontana, Enrico Baj and Bruno Munari. After making jewellery in silver and gold, he started sculpting abstract geometric volumes in lead, copper and bronze, excavating their surfaces with poetic, machine-like etchings. His work was featured at the 1967 Montréal Expo and his public art commissioned for the United Nations in New York and UNESCO in Paris.

Pomodoro's apartment is privately owned, but his work can be seen in Milan at the Arnaldo Pomodoro Foundation, established in 1995 at the artist's former studio. The foundation operates access to the enigmatic *Ingresso nel Labirinto* (1995–2011): Pomodoro's underground, postmodern sculptural environment inspired by the *Epic of Gilgamesh.*

In the 1960s, Sottsass was a leading player on Milan's design scene, which was moving away from Modernism's austerity towards injections of colour, emotion and symbolism. He pioneered

playful designs of calculators and typewriters for manufacturer Olivetti and invented other ingenious interior schemes such as a hybrid 'Tower' for Mario Tchou's apartment in 1963.

For his friend lithographer and printer Giovanni Lana, Sottsass designed the Casa Lana in 1965, a wooden cabin of cubes unfolding into a miniature space-saving architecture (a faithful reconstruction of which is permanently installed at the Triennale di Milano).

Sottsass's characterful solutions to compact urban living were internationally recognised in the landmark exhibition 'Italy: The New Domestic Landscape' at the Museum of Modern Art in 1972, and his multi-functional 'Carlton Room Divider' of 1981 is an icon of the Memphis movement, which he co-founded in 1980.

ABOVE AND OVERLEAF
Casa Lana's reconstruction at the Triennale di Milano.

13

The Bauhaus Masters' Houses

Dessau, Germany

Three pairs of semi-detached houses on the Bauhaus campus were home to artists such as Paul Klee, Wassily Kandinsky, Anni Albers and Lucia Moholy.

A perk of teaching on the faculty of the Bauhaus school in Dessau was moving into one of the 'Masters' Houses'. The three pairs of semi-detached houses designated for six department heads and their families were designed by founder of the school Walter Gropius (1883–1969). Just a short walk from the school, in a small pine wood, here artists and designers could live out the modern utopian dream that the Bauhaus propagated.

Artists were taught to apply their skills to industry and craft across a variety of workshops – from wood and metalworking, textile weaving, stained glass, graphics, furniture-making and architecture – uniting expression into one optimistic 'modern language' defined by colour theory and geometric shapes informed by industry, through which a new progressive society could emerge. The Masters' Houses, their interiors, fittings and furniture, all made in the Bauhaus workshops, were exemplary.

Formed of simple geometric white volumes of concrete, steel and glass, the two-storey houses each contain two residences, with mirroring floorplans. Living and dining on the ground floor; then on the first floor, bedrooms, bathrooms and a studio. Roofs were flat and interiors illuminated by daylight. They evolved from a prototype established by the Haus Am Horn (1923) in Weimar, where the Bauhaus was originally founded in 1919.

The school had moved to Dessau near Berlin in 1925, with the support of better municipal funding and a more liberal community. Using his experience in office and factory buildings, Gropius designed the whole campus: the school building – with workshops, offices, a canteen and auditorium – student accommodation, and his own 'Director's House' next to the Masters' Houses.

Over the years the school was in session, the Masters' Houses were inhabited by artists Paul Klee and Wassily Kandinsky; Georg Muche and Oskar Schlemmer; Lyonel Feininger, László Moholy-Nagy and Lucia Moholy. Then Josef and Anni Albers, Gertrud and Alfred Arndt, and Hinnerk Scheper. Each resident personalised the space with furniture or colour schemes, expanding their ideas

OPPOSITE
Staircase inside the Kandinsky/Klee House.

into three dimensions and into life itself.

As National Socialism gained momentum in Germany, the Nazis closed down the Bauhaus in 1933, with plans to fully eradicate the Modern style of architecture from Dessau, though heavy Allied bombing during World War II would get there first. After German unification, restoration work began in the 1990s, and in 1996 the Bauhaus (including the Masters' Houses) gained UNESCO World Heritage Site status. The campus is open to the public to visit and the Director's House was rebuilt in 2014 in a contemporary interpretation by architecture studio Bruno Fioretti Marquez.

LEFT
A room in Klee's side of the house.

ABOVE
The Kandinsky/Klee House.

Formed of geometric white volumes of concrete, steel and glass, the two-storey Masters' Houses each contain two residences, with mirroring floorplans.

14

Kurt Schwitters

Hannover, Germany

Built out of modernity's waste, the 'Merzbau' is an abstract living grotto that endures in concept through a museum reconstruction.

German artist and poet Kurt Schwitters (1887–1948) made abstract collaged constructions out of the found debris of modern life – newspapers, tickets, cigarette stubs, string, nails – which he named 'Merz'. In 1923, he began assembling a 'Merzbau' (Merz-building) inside his house and studio in Hannover: the immersive, dimensional collage grew into an architecture over 16 years, eventually encompassing eight rooms.

Schwitters studied art in Hannover and Dresden, and after serving as a draughtsman during World War I, he enrolled to study architecture, though instead began experimenting in Expressionist and Cubist art. Through his 'Merzbau', he fused the 'Neo-plastic' language of Constructivism and De Stijl (which influenced Dada and the Bauhaus) with found waste materials – recycling and transforming old into new.

When, in 1937, his radical work was included in the Nazi regime's Degenerate Art Exhibition, he followed his son into exile in Norway, where he built a second, two-storey Merzbau just outside Oslo (destroyed by fire in 1951). When the Nazis invaded Norway in 1940 he left to England, where he began the third Merzbau in the Lake District in 1947 (partially preserved by the University of Newcastle at the Hatton Gallery).

The original Hannover Merzbau was destroyed by Allied bombing in 1943, but its main room was reconstructed in the 1980s into a permanent installation at the city's Sprengel Museum. Stage designer Peter Bissegger rebuilt it to scale, assisted by photographs taken in 1933 and the memory of the artist's son Ernst Schwitters.

What cannot be replicated is the Merzbau's continuous state of accumulative growth, as a product of the inhabitant's material waste. Schwitters criticised Modern architecture for how it prioritised universal function over local adaptation to contexts from climate to personality, using the cutting-edge Weissenhof Estate in Stuttgart – designed by leading architects such as Walter Gropius, Mies van der Rohe and Le Corbusier – as a case in point. His psychological reading of waste and its re-use has gained new meaning today.

OPPOSITE
The reconstructed Merzbau at the Sprengel Museum in Hannover.

15 Hermann Rosa

Munich, Germany

This self-built Brutalist concrete architecture was an extension of the artist's disciplined sculptural process and way of life.

German sculptor Hermann Rosa (1911–1981) designed and constructed his studio in Munich in the 1960s. Built of exposed concrete and glass, the light-filled, minimalist frame aligned with the Brutalist architectural movement, which explored the sculptural qualities of raw concrete from the 1950s.

The son of a stonemason, Rosa was born in the region of Saxony. He studied stonemasonry and then art in Prague, where he gained recognition, met his wife Maria Panz, and aligned with a politically socialist and communist community. After the annexation of Czechoslovakian Sudetenland to Germany in 1938, Rosa returned home. After being interned by the Nazis for his political views, he found an apprenticeship in Dresden under artist Karl Albiker. Both shared an interest in the modern paintings of Cézanne and distanced themselves from the regime.

After the war, Rosa moved to Munich, where an anti-Modern atmosphere still prevailed since the Nazi eradication of liberal arts. He worked on a sculptural style informed by Giacometti, making experimental raw busts from portraits, working in two different studios in the 1950s that he also self-built. The process of building was an extension of his sculptural practice: disciplined, iterative, meaningful and human.

His third self-built studio in Schwabing took around eight years to construct, completing in 1968 – with help from wood sculptor Ludwig Spegel, and his wife and son. The concrete building has two steel-framed walls of windows, a flattened gable roof pierced with an oculus skylight, and a floating concrete staircase leading up to a mezzanine level.

The concrete was poured into a wooden-board formwork bringing a textured patina to the walls. Pipes and electrics were inset into the structure and left exposed, and wooden benches were integrated. In 1968, a separate bathroom building, chimney and later a basement were added, connected by stepping stones through the garden. The complex was heritage-protected as a national monument in 1988.

OPPOSITE
The artist's studio.

Modern Art Meets the Modern House

What was the relationship between Modern art and Modern domestic architecture in the 20th century?

Modern art and architecture movements developed closely, yet also on their own distinct trajectories, across the 20th century. Modern art, after all, is a fairly immediate and individual form of expression, while architecture is slow and collaborative – buildings take budgets, resources and planning permissions to complete. Artists are known to be reactive, perhaps more emotional and imaginative, whereas architects are considered more measured, deliberate and grounded in their personality types.

In the 20th century, as many of these houses show, the two mediums reached a reciprocal relationship that was sometimes mutually idealistic and at other times critical and disruptive. Both mediums reflected the themes of 'modernity' defined by urbanisation, social change, technology and consumerism – one through subjects and concepts, the other through materials and lifestyles.

Rice Pereira, Oblique Progression, 1948.

The genesis of Modern art in Europe is generally understood to root itself in the late 19th century with the emergence of Realism and Impressionism. Artists began exploring everyday subjects in artistic styles distinct to their own unique viewpoints and emotions, rather than using historical and religious subjects in canonical styles of the past. Informed by a plethora of influences from travel to photography, these new ways of thinking and seeing permeated artistic expression across the world in the 20th century.

In Europe in the 1920s and 30s, subjects were being distilled into mathematical geometric abstraction where things seemed to make more sense (Cubism, Purism, Constructivism, De Stijl, Neo-Plasticism) – or in the other direction, descending into seductive yet nightmarish realms where nothing made sense (Surrealism and Dada). In their own ways, constructing or deconstructing, both responded to the devastation and disruption of World War I (1914–18).

During this time, many artists were working across the spectrum between constructing and deconstructing and outside prescribed movements – with individual and geographic perspectives that still held the characteristics of Modern viewpoints, styles and thinking: examples in this book include Tamara de Lempicka, Frida Kahlo or Fumio Asakura.

So, while on some canvases clocks and tree-trunks were melting, other canvases began to look like architectural blueprints reflecting the rhythmic new language of the mechanised and electrifying 'Machine Age'. Here is where art met architecture in its closest mutually appreciative relationship of the 20th century: the Bauhaus school operating from 1919–1933 in Germany, first in Weimar, then Dessau.

The school brought together art and architecture – as well as design and craft – under one non-hierarchical umbrella with the aim of rebuilding a utopian, functional lifestyle after World War I. Modern artistic contributions of colour theory and aesthetic balance contributed vitally to Bauhaus architecture, defined by collections of cube-like volumes with large windows, flat roofs and terraces, within which furniture was smoothly integrated. It expressed a newly improved way of life that was clean, bright and smooth. (1)

In Paris, Le Corbusier interpreted the language of Modern architecture with his 'Five Points' of 1923 that comprised: pilotis, integrating open-air spaces into closed volumes; the flat roof terrace, bringing more outdoor living space; the free plan, opening up the interior plan for open-ended possibilities; the free facade, allowing a building to be sculpted to its context; and windows that maximize light, views and privacy. (2) (See the 'Purist' studio-houses of Amédée Ozenfant, entry 7, and René Guiette, entry 22.)

While Modern Architecture was already in development from the late 19th century, the work of Le Corbusier and the Bauhaus school are generally recognised as the nucleus of the movement in Europe, which followed on from Art Nouveau and Art Deco,

While on some canvases clocks and tree-trunks were melting, other canvases began to look like architectural blueprints.

informed by innovations in steel and concrete engineering, from lessons learned from factories and skyscrapers, and the flow of ideas between Europe and America. (3)

As well as travel, it was conflict, colonialism and war that dispersed the ideas of Modern Art and Architecture in the mid-20th century. As the Nazis strengthened their foothold in Germany in the run-up to World War II (1939–45), they sought to eliminate both expressions, degrading artists in 'degenerate exhibitions' and closing the Bauhaus School down. (4) Architecture in general slowed down during wartime years due to lack of resources, labour and materials.

Artists and architects with Jewish heritage fled Germany, then many other countries in Europe as the Nazis occupied them, seeking safety abroad. In this book you will follow Tamara de Lempicka to New York; Marguerite Wildenhain to California; Bernat Klein to Britain; and Erwin Broner to Ibiza. Many other artists were affected: Kurt Schwitters left Hannover for Oslo then Britain; Sophie Taeuber-Arp left the house she designed in Paris, never to return; and Barbara Hepworth settled in Cornwall to stay safe. In the US, Japanese American artists Ruth Asawa and Isamu Noguchi were imprisoned in camps as a consequence of Japan's entry into the war.

After the war, Modern Architecture re-emerged with a solid and very real new purpose: reconstruction and mass social housing. The ideas established for single-family houses were expanded to an urban scale, to varying degrees of success. Beyond Europe and the US, countries were breaking free from colonial ties, resulting in post-independence movements that re-evaluated Modernism in the context of nationalism: see Ena De Silva (see entry 35) and Demas Nwoko (entry 33).

The colonial period, which had begun in the 15th century, had resulted in new objects entering Europe and America from abroad – from batik textiles, to Ukiyo-e and the traditional artefacts of Indigenous cultures – all of which had a great influence on the aesthetics of Modern Art throughout the 20th century, from pattern to perspective and form.

Early Modernist architecture had been inspired by technology and mass production, designed to be rolled out and replicated across cultures with the same universal meaning and function. Yet, the repercussions of this were starting to be seen by the 1950s: mental displacement, a loss of humanity and therefore care and belonging.

Modernism had to find a balance between an open, liberating international flow, while preserving the complexity and beauty of place and culture – later written about by Kenneth Frampton in his theory of Critical Regionalism in the 1980s. Regional approaches to Modernism can be seen in the work of Josep Lluís Sert in Mallorca, Juan O'Gorman in Mexico and the house of Oswaldo Guayasamín in Quito, who all introduced Indigenous shape, colour and landscape design into their Modern buildings.

It was the specifics of climate and environment that equally drove these later regional blends of Modernism. In tropical climates, the timeless know-how of vernacular architecture developed over centuries was crucial to incorporate into new functional styles of living (for example, ancient techniques for cooling and ventilation were central to Bawa and Nwoko's designs). In Ibiza, artist and architect Broner studied the similarities between vernacular and Modernism, ideas that were explored in the seminal 'Architecture Without Architects' MoMA exhibition in 1964 curated by Bernard Rudofsky, which reappraised vernacular. (5)

We do not yet live in a virtual techno-utopia, yet today artists do live in houses that do not physically exist.

Modernism wasn't all about machines. Conversely, many Modern artists – Hans Arp, Marta Pan and Barbara Hepworth, for instance – were informed by natural, organic forms throughout the century, perhaps as a form of grounding or escapism from, or even rebellion and protest to the changing world. So were Modern architects, which leads us to the examples of mid-century West Coast Modernism that favoured wood for construction rather than steel and concrete. These were influenced in form by local vernacular and the ideas of influential American architect Frank Lloyd Wright and his integration of architecture with nature and landscape, developing around the same time as Le Corbusier in Paris.

Wood expressed warmth and an organic quality opposite in character to steel and concrete. The simple, economic yet sensual beauty of wooden Modern houses can be seen in those by Arthur Erickson in West Vancouver, who was inspired by Japanese architecture; also in those of artists Gordon Onslow Ford (entry 45) and Marguerite Wildenhain (entry 38) in Northern California; the summer cabin of Irma Salo Jæger (entry 28) in Denmark; or the pragmatic coastal complex of Sigurjón Ólafsson (entry 29) in Iceland.

Meanwhile, by the 1960s, New York had become the capital of Modern Art. Abstract Expressionism translated raw emotions into actions, canvases were attacked, slapped and sloshed with paint, capturing the chaos and energy of the modern city. The Civil Rights Movement inspired Modern art, communicating Black pride through the Black Arts Movement, the activist Spiral group formed in 1963, the opening of the Studio Museum in Harlem in 1968 and, in the 1970s, the influential gallery Just Above Midtown.

On the other hand, there was Minimalism, represented in this book by Donald Judd (entry 43), who distilled forms into light and geometry: he saw beauty in the purity of factory floors being converted by artists into loft apartments from the 1950s when industry was leaving New York City and industrial buildings were being demolished. Judd saw potential in their large open spaces for exhibiting art, living without boundaries, and hosting gatherings for artists.

The post-war modern city, predominantly constructed of concrete, became a new stage for performance; an endless subject for photography that captured powerfully geometric shadows and colliding social dynamics; and its brutal rawness translated into sculpture and art. This can be seen from the 1950s in the Gutai movement (translated as 'concreteness') in Japan, or the Neo-Concrete movement in the rapidly urbanising Brazilian cities of São Paulo and Rio de Janeiro.

The application and experimentation with concrete resulted in a global embrace of Brutalism, the movement in which architects sculpted béton brut (raw concrete) like artists, creating absorbing spaces and bold silhouettes. The Metabolists in Japan took this a step further fusing the aesthetics of steel and concrete engineering with the organic structures of nature.

In the 1970s, the original ideas of Modern Art and Modern Architecture were existent yet diluting, blending and evolving with the strengthening of mass production and consumerism. Visually this was in the form of the growing power and presence of advertisements and branding. Architecturally, the increasing speed of prefabrication and information meant that buildings were constructed more quickly and at decreasing quality, replicated, banal, rolled out across suburban landscapes – another consumable object to own rather than a crafted, cultural place of being.

This prevailing mood seems very pessimistic – but there was joy in reinvention and rethinking the solutions. In 1972, 'The New Domestic Landscape' exhibition at MoMA captured the spirit of the moment through playful examples of Radical Italian design. (6) It was divided into two camps: counter-design and pro-design. The former was deconstructive and anti-capitalist, while the latter was constructive and capitalist. On the one hand living spaces were reduced to grids, mirrors, tubes, wires, screens and speakers; and on the other, Ettore Sottsass exhibited clever Tardis-like capsule 'micro-environments' on castors (ideas of which you can see in entry 12) – functionalising small living spaces in cities to make life uber-convenient.

The same spirit can be seen in Postmodernism (see Charles Vandenhove, entry 23, and Edgardo Giménez, entry 50) and Pop Art – bouncing off colour, kitsch, consumerism and populist forms of Classical architecture. Rather than the house, the city, the skyscraper or the factory, it was now the era of leisure and entertainment, freedom and fantasy; the mood was neither constructive nor deconstructive; after the rollercoaster ride of the 20th century so far, it had become blissfully and perhaps dangerously ambivalent, chasing quick thrills, and generally taking itself less seriously.

Finally, both Modern Art and Modern Architecture retreated from the physical and into the Information Age, showing a mere few of its founding values. Fluxus and later Post-Internet art took place on screens and in virtual games, accompanied by architectural movements that echoed digital structures and forms only possible with computer-aided design: High-Tech (think the Centre Pompidou in Paris) explored ideas of infinite and temporary structures, while Deconstructivism (think Zaha Hadid and Daniel Libeskind) tested the limits of reality.

Here we can conclude that Modern Art and Modern Architecture went through various phases of agreeing and disagreeing – like in any great relationship, they inspired each other, were critical, then embraced change and evolution. While we separate the training of the two disciplines, it's clear that many artists across the 20th century thought architecturally, and many architects thought like artists. Every individual in this book is multi-dimensional – often working across disciplines from fashion, interiors, art, craft and landscape design and integrating each with 'Modern' approaches.

We do not yet live in a virtual techno-utopia, yet today artists do live in houses that do not physically exist – in online communities, in virtual portfolios, in creative networks, in archives that live on the cloud – and that maybe are stronger than physical ones, and unsusceptible to destruction as many houses of the past have been, especially in our 21st-century context of climate emergency. Yet we also still live with and cherish 'modernity' (the lessons and discoveries of the Modern Age) in our lives; just as artists and architects continue to work within the styles, aesthetics and theories of Modernism – recognising and rejecting the flaws of the past and taking the qualities of function, humanity, idealism and cosmopolitanism forward.

16

Salvador Dalí

Portlligat, Spain

A simple fisherman's hut by the sea evolved into a theatrical reflection of the artist's inner psyche infused with Surrealism and Pop Art.

In 1930 Spanish Surrealist artist Salvador Dalí (1904–1989) bought a fisherman's hut in the village of Portlligat, north-east of Barcelona. Drawn to the landscape, the light and isolation, he lived there with his wife and muse Gala for 40 years. During this time, they organically expanded the house according to their instincts and eccentricities.

The architecture follows the traditional local vernacular with rough-plastered, whitewashed walls and terracotta floors, yet its 'modernity' lies in its embodiment of the Modern Art movement of Surrealism. It was in Paris in the mid-1920s that Dalí first encountered the Surrealists, who explored dreams and the subconscious informed by the ideas of the founder of psychoanalysis Sigmund Freud.

During his early years at the house, Dalí painted some of his most celebrated works made under his 'paranoiac critical' hallucinatory state. Distorted objects and metaphoric symbols emerged within ethereal landscapes – many inspired by Portlligat.

It seems like the house evolved in a similar way, spontaneously forming into a labyrinth of womb-like rooms, curving corridors and freeform niches. The couple filled it with kitsch antiques, rustic furniture, velvet upholstery, stuffed animals, books, candles and dried flowers. Pop Art scenery surrounded the courtyard pool: swan sculptures, a pink-lips sofa, plastic Pirelli tyres and a telephone booth.

Soon Dalí fell out of favour with the Surrealists due to his political ambivalence to the rise of fascism, and he began painting in an Italian Renaissance-inspired style. In 1936, due to the Spanish Civil War, Dalí and Gala left for Paris, and then to America during World War II, where Dalí worked on designing stage sets and shop interiors.

In 1948 they returned to the house at Portlligat. In the same region, Dalí began creating the theatrical Dalí Theatre-Museum and 12th-century Gothic 'Gala Dalí Castle'. Today, all three places are owned by the Dalí Foundation and possible to visit for a strange and surreal adventure into the mind of the artist.

OPPOSITE
A surreal egg balanced on the Portlligat house.

17

Joan Miró | Josep Lluís Sert

Mallorca, Spain

Adjoining the artist's home, the 'Sert Studio' fused Bauhaus design with Mediterranean spirit in an expression of Catalan Modernism.

When Barcelona-born artist Joan Miró (1893–1983) settled in Mallorca with his wife Pilar Juncosa, who was from the island, he was a successful artist in his mid-sixties. Seeking a creative refuge, he bought an estate near Palma. His brother-in-law Enric Juncosa built them a house and a studio was designed by his friend, Spanish architect Josep Lluís Sert (1902–1983), who had studied architecture in Barcelona and apprenticed under Le Corbusier in Paris.

The two-storey studio combined Bauhaus-inspired Modernism with Mediterranean spirit. Concrete meets local vernacular materials of stone, clay bricks and terracotta. The facade displays a bright colour scheme of red, yellow and blue panels and doors, and it is topped with a sculpturally vaulted roof – geometric yet organic, nodding to the work of Gaudí and the Casa Fajol by Josep Graner i Prat in Barcelona.

There, Miró worked in the ground-floor, double-height studio on multiple large canvases. His style had reached maturity, combining elements of Surrealism, Dada and Cubism, yet finding its own language of bold colours, free lines and vivid symbols of stars, musical notes, birds and insects. A sliding door separates a storage area, and on a mezzanine level he kept postcards, photographs, shells, stones and Mediterranean folk objects.

Sert was a key figure of Catalan Modernism in Barcelona in the 1930s, co-designing the Spanish Republican Pavilion for the Paris World's Fair in 1937, for which artists Miró, Alexander Calder and Pablo Picasso contributed works. After the Spanish Civil War, in 1939 the Franco dictatorship drove Sert into exile in the United States, where he became a professor of architecture at Harvard University. Miró left for Paris, and spent the following wartime years between Mallorca, Barcelona and his Catalan farm Mont-roig – before retreating, after ten busy post-war years, to Mallorca in 1955 as an in-demand artist.

With Sert in the US, the pair worked on the studio's design by post, sending letters and drawings back and forth over two years, with Enric supervising construction. The result united Modernism

OPPOSITE
A detail of the studio facade showing its rhythmic geometry.

RIGHT
The facade of white concrete and traditional local materials.

Artist and architect worked on the studio's design by post, sending letters and drawings back and forth over two years.

with humanism, landscape and a sublime experience of light – inspiring two further temples to art by Sert: the Fondation Maeght in Saint Paul de Vence in 1964 (commissioned by Miró's dealer Aimé Maeght) and the Fundació Joan Miró in Barcelona in 1975.

In 1981, Miró established the Fundació Miró Mallorca and gifted the Sert Studio to the city of Palma. Today, its original atmosphere has been preserved alongside the neighbouring 18th-century 'Son Boter' finca, decorated with Miró's murals. A museum and sculpture garden complete the artist's cultural campus.

18

Xavier Corberó

Barcelona, Spain

The Espai Corberó blurs the lines between fantasy folly and artists' community with a design that blends Surrealism and Brutalism.

On the outskirts of Barcelona, Catalan sculptor Xavier Corberó (1935–2017) built a fantastical architectural structure of more than 300 stacked and colonnaded concrete arches that became his home, studio, an artists' community and obsession. It all began in 1968, when he purchased a compound of land and after renovating an old house, he just kept on building without plans for over five decades, right up until his death.

Named the Espai Corberó, the sprawling labyrinth of nine buildings is interwoven with a dozen courtyards inhabited by ponds, plants and Corberó's monolithic sculptures: bold, natural forms hewn of rough stone, marble and bronze. Inside, there are studios, living spaces, ten bedrooms and a vast columnless underground theatre with a vaulted ceiling.

Corberó came from a family of artists, designers and metalworkers. His father worked at his grandfather's bronze foundry, and co-founded the art school Escola Massana in Barcelona. The city was a creative place to be in the 1950s and 60s, and he met characters such as Ricardo Bofill, Salvador Dalí (who is said to have bought Corberó's first work of art), Joan Miró and Josep Lluís Sert. He also travelled to New York, where he met Marcel Duchamp, Max Ernst and Man Ray, and later in the 1970s, monumental sculptors Claes Oldenburg and Richard Serra.

Rather than a house or studio, Corberó imagined a psychological architecture that could unlock the spiritual, mystical and emotional. It defied categorisation, blurring the lines between function and folly, public and private, personal and community-oriented. Inspired by the Bauhaus, in 1972 he established the Center for Artistic Activities and Research of Catalonia (CAIAC), welcoming artists and artisans to use the space as a workshop.

Now owned by the local municipality, Espai Corberó seems to have pre-empted the aesthetic of computer-generated fantasy worlds with its repetitive composition overground by nature. It is the artist's most renowned work: a scene from a Surrealist painting, an inhabitable abstract sculpture, and a poetic Brutalist landscape.

OPPOSITE
The arches of the Espai Corberó.

Corberó imagined a psychological architecture that could unlock the spiritual, mystical and emotional.

19

Erwin Broner

Ibiza, Spain

Blending Bauhaus with the wisdom of local Ibizan vernacular, this house and studio is a creative retreat overlooking the sea.

German artist, designer and architect Erwin Broner (1898–1971) studied at the Bauhaus and later, in 1959, when he was in his early sixties, ended up settling in Ibiza. Inspired by the simple beauty and economy of the local 'finca', he built his own house, blending Modernism with traditional vernacular materials and construction knowledge – finding many similarities between the two.

As a German Jew, Broner left Germany in 1933 after Hitler came to power, travelling first to Barcelona, then Ibiza, among a group of other artists and intellectuals including Walter Benjamin, Albert Camus and Man Ray. When he arrived on the island, he connected deeply with its magic, yet left in 1936 when the Spanish Civil War broke out: first to New York, then Hollywood, where he worked as a set designer and photographer, and then to Mexico with his third wife Gisela.

He always dreamed of returning to Ibiza to paint and live, which eventually happened when in the early 1960s he bought a plot of land overlooking the sea. His house is a white, top-heavy concrete cube, set over two levels with a roof terrace and integrated into the slope of the land. Upstairs, the open-plan living space has large windows and opens up to a sheltered loggia terrace, while the large glass doors of the lower floor open up to nature and views of the sea.

As well as concrete, there are warm local materials: terracotta tiles, exposed dry stone walls and wooden shutters. In the Bauhaus style, he designed every piece of furniture using his design and carpentry skills, often opting for folding elements and castors for easy rearrangement. Chair backrests were specially angled to the sea view and lamps were made of wood with paper shades.

OPPOSITE
The stepped house is built into the sloping land.

Broner designed around thirty Modernist houses, both new constructions and renovations, on Ibiza and Formentera.

White-painted concrete meets terracotta tiles, wooden shutters and dry stone walls.

Broner was an active participant in the local art scene, founding the Ibiza 59 group with fellow German artists on the island. Based at the El Corsario gallery, they invited other abstract artists to the island such as Hans Hartung, Pierre Soulages and Jean Dubuffet. Overall as an architect he designed around thirty modern houses, both new constructions and renovations, on Ibiza and Formentera – as well as proposing planning solutions to public issues from waste management to public baths.

In 2000, his widow Gisela donated Casa Broner to Ibiza, and in 2011, after restoration and six years after Gisela's death, it opened to the public as a house museum, displaying his books, furniture and objects. His abstract paintings of free shapes in warm Mediterranean colour palettes are held in Ibiza's Museum of Contemporary Art collection.

OPPOSITE
The living room with a traditional fireplace.

20

Antoni Tàpies | Josep Antoni Coderch

Barcelona, Spain

Behind this rhythmic, geometric facade lies a layered urban house unfolding an introspective artistic laboratory.

This narrow urban house and studio in Barcelona's Sant Gervasi district was built in 1960 for Catalan artist Antoni Tàpies (1923–2012), designed by Barcelona native, architect Josep Antoni Coderch (1913–1984). Its rhythmic rectangular shutters are a geometric contrast to more traditional neighbours – and behind them lies an introspective laboratory of an artistic life oriented around a lush courtyard garden.

Balancing privacy and daylight, the facade of prefabricated fibre-cement panels and white-painted slatted shutters mediates between the street and the house. Entry through the wide door leads past a small caretaker's residence, beyond which lies the internal courtyard and double-height studio with pyramidal skylights.

With sections of exposed brick walls, the stacked living spaces are connected by a central staircase. The first floor features kitchen, dining and living areas; the second floor, the bedrooms; and above this, the rooftop library where Tàpies would read and write is lined with bookcases and intersected by a black metal fireplace.

Tàpies taught himself to paint during the challenging years of the Spanish Civil War (1936–39). In 1948 he co-founded Dau al Set, a magazine published until 1956 that set out to revive the pre-war Catalan avant-garde represented by Dalí and Miró. By the mid-1950s, Tàpies had gained recognition for his textured, abstract canvases that mixed marble dust with paint and layered informal materials of clay, paper and waste textiles, later integrating signs and symbols.

During the civil war, architect Coderch had returned to Spain from Germany where he had been apprenticing. He served as a supplementary officer on the Nationalist side. Interested in architects such as Josep Lluís Sert, who fused Modernism with local traditions and materials, he co-founded 'Group R' in 1951, as an extension of 'GATCPAC', the earlier group of Catalan Modernists.

The same year, Coderch designed the Spanish Pavilion for the Triennale di Milano – a politically tense commission due to the Franco dictatorship. His design sought to unify art, modernity and Mediterranean tradition through references to Ibizan vernacular

ABOVE
The shuttered facade of the house.

architecture, and works by Gaudí and Miró, as well as architectural elements such as the screen facade, courtyards and exposed natural materials.

In 1984, artist Tàpies established the Fundació Antoni Tàpies in Barcelona, seeking to highlight the centrality of art to modernity and its progression. The Tàpies Museum opened in 1990, in an early example of Catalan Modernism, a pioneering 19th-century former publishing house designed by architect Lluís Domènech i Montaner in Eixample.

21

César Manrique

Lanzarote, Spain

Inspired by the volcanic landscape, this artist invented a regional Modernist architectural style for Lanzarote, where he designed himself two houses.

Spanish artist César Manrique (1919–1992) was born on the Canary Island of Lanzarote, a place where he pioneered a local artistic and architectural aesthetic informed by the dark volcanic rocks, the wind and the resilient plants of the island's sub-tropical desert landscapes. During his lifetime, he lived in two houses on the island that he designed himself, the Volcano House and the Palm Grove house.

Manrique grew up on the island, yet after volunteering as a teenager in the Spanish Civil War on the Nationalist side, he moved to Madrid in 1945 to study art, after briefly exploring architecture. In 1964 he moved to New York, then in 1966 – at the age of 47, and in the midst of international success as an artist – he moved back to the remote, relatively underdeveloped island of his birth where water shortages were common and agriculture was sparse. After travelling the world, he saw the island with a new appreciation.

Manrique's first work of architecture on Lanzarote was the Jameos del Agua, an arts and culture centre, which inhabits the natural volcanic rock with an organic-shaped pool of white-painted concrete and cave auditorium. In 1968, he converted five underground air bubbles beneath a field of petrified lava into the Volcano House in Tahiche where he lived for 20 years. The volcanic rock seems to flow inside through the windows and today it is home to the César Manrique Foundation.

As tourism increased in Lanzarote, Manrique moved north to the town of Haría in 1988, where he would spend the last years of his life. He converted a farmhouse into a Modernist house of connected white cubes, surrounded by palm trees. This would later become the César Manrique House Museum, opened in 2013, which has preserved his artist's studio as he left it complete with oil paints, sketches and unfinished works.

Manrique continued to make architectural interventions into the landscape, including the Mirador del Río in 1973 and the Jardín de Cactus, which opened in 1991. Manrique died in a car accident in 1992 and shortly afterwards his architectural work was recognized by UNESCO for its innovative and artistic integration of human and environmental habitats.

OPPOSITE
Lagomar, a house designed by Cesar Manrique.

OVERLEAF
The artist's studio (left) and the living space interior (right) at the Palm Grove house.

Picasso 1881 · 1981
AELE - BIOSCA - EGAM - GRUPO 15 - KREISLER DOS
JUANA MORDO - MULTIPLE 4.17 - THEO - VANDRES
MADRID - ENERO - DICIEMBRE 1981

PICASSO

ABOVE
The Volcano House.

The artist converted five underground air bubbles beneath a field of petrified lava into the Volcano House.

22

René Guiette | Le Corbusier

Antwerp, Belgium

An early example of Modern architecture in Belgium, this radical white box is stacked with function and a spatial colour scheme.

Belgian artist and art critic René Guiette (1893–1976) visited Le Corbusier's 'Pavillon de L'Esprit Nouveau' at the progressive International Exposition of Decorative and Industrial Arts in 1925. He was drawn to the cubic white architecture carved of functional voids and grids of windows, inspired by the modern way of life it encouraged. He decided he wanted one for himself, and commissioned Le Corbusier and his cousin Pierre Jeanneret to design the Maison Guiette in Antwerp, built in 1927.

The son of Belgian 19th-century artist Jules Guiette, René started painting in 1919 after serving in World War I. He experimented with Expressionism and Cubism, enriched by the ideas of his friend René Magritte, then later developed a style similar to Jean Dubuffet's 'Art Brut' inspired by calligraphy and esotericism.

Considered one of the first examples of Modern architecture in Belgium, the Maison Guiette is a radical white box located on a narrow plot. Like the Ozenfant studio-house (see entry 7), this two-storey house belongs to Le Corbusier's Purist period, following many elements of his 'Five Points' of Modern Architecture published in 1923 – including the large windows, open interior plan and flat roof and terrace.

The ground-floor living spaces and office open up to the garden. On the first floor are the bedrooms and bathrooms, and on the second floor there is a nursery, double-height artist's studio (illuminated by the large, gridded window on the front facade), a dark room for photographic development, housekeeper's room and a little balcony.

Influenced by Purist art, which evolved from Cubism, Le Corbusier used colour to shape the emotional atmosphere of the house. Bright colours make the narrow spaces appear larger and lighter while contrasts of white with blue, ochre, pink, green and grey structure and segment the interiors.

The house and studio was heritage-protected in 1978 after plans for a motorway left it at risk of demolition. Belgian fashion designer Ann Demeulemeester bought the house in 1983 and it was restored by architect George Baines. In 2016, it was added to UNESCO's World Heritage List alongside other works by Le Corbusier.

OPPOSITE
Maison Guiette.

23 Léon Wuidar | Charles Vandenhove

Liège, Belgium

Classicism meets Brutalism at this 1970s Postmodern house, born from a reciprocal relationship between artist and architect.

The house of Belgian artist Léon Wuidar (b. 1938) was designed by Belgian architect Charles Vandenhove (1927–2019) in 1974. The pair first admired each other's work, then became friends and later collaborators. The house and studio – designed in exchange for paintings – combined modern materials such as exposed concrete bricks with Classical forms such as the triangular pediment and arches. While Postmodern in style, its economy embraces Brutalism – the mid-century movement that embraced the sculptural qualities of béton brut (raw concrete).

Born in Liège, Wuidar grew up surrounded by the urban destruction of post-war Belgium. A self-taught painter and drawing teacher since 1959, he explored figuration yet found his style in 1963 in a flat minimalist abstraction juxtaposing precise shapes and bold colours, informed by Bauhaus artist Paul Klee (see entry 13). From the 1970s, he embraced a new dimensionality that echoed architectural blueprints, windows and roofs.

In the 1960s Wuidar established a friendship with modern architect Vandenhove, who also lived in Liège, and asked him to design a house with total creative freedom. Set across one level, the house that emerged has a vaulted roof with stepped gables, informed by Vandenhove's visit to Andrea Palladio's 16th-century Villa Foscari in Italy.

Inside, there is a basilica-style plan of five bays around a long central space – three for family living, one for the entrance and the last for a workshop. Nature is framed by the large arched windows and the coffered ceiling casts shifting patterns of shadows. Colourful, site-specific paintings are displayed on the walls and Vandenhove designed the cabinets and lighting fixtures.

The pair collaborated on other projects together including the University Hospital of Liège, and Wuidar designed a ceiling mural of repetitive triangles for Vandenhove's own home and studio, the restored 16th-century Torrentius Hotel.

Across his career, Vandenhove commissioned many other artists for his buildings: Sol LeWitt, Daniel Buren, Anne and Patrick Poirier to name a few. Subsequently, Wuidar worked with other

ABOVE
One of the interior bays.

Wuidar found his artistic style in a flat minimalist abstraction juxtaposing precise shapes and bold colours.

ABOVE
The exterior facade with arched pediment window.

architects – such as André Jacqmain, Roger Bastin, Claude Strebelle and Helmut Schiffiers.

In 1995, Vandenhove expanded Wuidar's house with a three-level concrete box and spiral staircase. The artist lives in the house today, and the Torrentius Hotel, which houses the late architect's archive and extensive modern art collection (donated in part to the University of Ghent), can be visited through the Jeanne & Charles Vandenhove Foundation, established in 2004.

24

Floris Jespers | Léon Stynen, Huib Hoste

Antwerp, Belgium

From the late 1920s, the artist transformed his early 20th-century house with the help of some maverick Modernist architects.

Belgian artist Floris Jespers (1889–1965) commissioned several local Modern architects to transform his existing early 20th-century house and studio in Antwerp. Renovated and adapted between the 1920s and 50s, what emerged was a dynamic, light-filled house with an interior designed by Huib Hoste (1881–1957) and colourful murals on the walls. The collaborative house was a crossroads for ideas within the emerging Modernist movement in Antwerp.

Jespers was born in Antwerp and studied art there, becoming a key figure of the avant-garde – alongside the likes of Jozef Peeters, Jos Léonard and Paul Joostens. He embraced elements of Cubism, Constructivism and Expressionism, often working on large-scale murals and tapestries.

In 1927, he bought the Art Deco house, originally designed in 1909 by Eugène Geefs for his brother, the sculptor Georges Geefs. Seeking an architecture that reflected his own modern approach, he appointed prolific local architect Frits De Mont to transform the facade with a new layered geometry of red brick, grids of windows, steel and cement parapets. The interior was opened up and furnished with Huib Hoste's Constructivist daybeds, stools and dining set, and a bright-red and black twisting staircase was added.

Set across three storeys, the studio occupies the ground and second floor, with the living space on the first floor. In 1932, Jespers commissioned architect Léon Stynen (1899–1990) to remodel the ground-floor facade and plan, transforming it into a gallery with an S-shaped entrance with ribbon windows. In 1941, Stynen designed a rooftop extension but the plans were rejected by the occupying Nazis, yet in 1953 architect Jan Mol adapted it and also added a garage.

OPPOSITE
The facade by Frits De Mont.

The collaborative house was a crossroads for ideas within the emerging Modernist movement in Antwerp.

The current owners of the house celebrate its history; a five-year project from 2018 brought it back to life with the help of architects, craftspeople and restoration specialists. Some elements were reinterpreted using reclaimed materials, relevant to today and the post-war era. Other parts were carefully updated for contemporary life, including a new skylight above the staircase, raised mezzanine level and roof terrace.

The process revealed a series of hidden murals by Jespers, who used the walls like a practice canvas – upstairs, a huge energetic harbour setting is layered with seagulls, boats and architecture, all colliding in Cubist dimensions. The scene was described by Modernist poet Paul Van Ostaijen, Jespers' friend and regular visitor, in one of his poems. Downstairs, sections of further wall paintings depict brightly coloured abstracted portraits of women, informed by Jespers' later years in the Congo, and in the staircase, a fragment of a poem by Van Ostaijen.

ABOVE
The entrance by Léon Stynen.

OPPOSITE
The staircase by Huib Hoste.

25 Barbara Hepworth

St Ives, Cornwall, England

The artist lived and worked at the Trewyn Studio where she sculpted organic forms in open-air workshops surrounded by layered gardens.

In search of more space to work on her sculptures, British artist Barbara Hepworth (1903–75) moved into the Trewyn Studio in St Ives, Cornwall, in 1949. She gradually expanded the modest white house overlooking the bay with outdoor workshops, and it became her home in 1951. There, she worked on bronze, stone and wood-carving, surrounded by a verdant garden where she placed her organic, totemic sculptures.

Growing up in Yorkshire, Hepworth was inspired by the lines and shapes of the rolling landscape. She studied art in Leeds, then in London at the Royal College of Art alongside her contemporary, British sculptor Henry Moore. In 1932, she created her first 'pierced form' sculpture, a curved, natural shape with a hole inside it, a shape that would become representative of her aesthetic.

During these years she met her second husband, sculptor Ben Nicholson, and socialised with other modern artists including sculptor Naum Gabo and photographer Lee Miller. When war was imminent in 1939, Hepworth and Nicholson and their young family were were invited to stay with their friend Adrian Stokes near St Ives. They decided to remain there, joining a community of artists that included Patrick Heron and Bernard Leach. When her marriage ended, Hepworth moved into her studio.

Located on a residential road on Barnoon Hill, Trewyn Studio is a two-storey stone building with whitewashed walls and a pitched slate roof. At the back of the house, there are two mid-20th-century studios – an outhouse and a greenhouse with large doors opening onto a yard (the latter acquired from her neighbour, sculptor John Milne).

OPPOSITE AND NEXT PAGE
The garden studio workshops.

The Barbara Hepworth Museum and Sculpture Garden preserves the artist's atmosphere of creation.

The garden was designed with help from Hepworth's friend, composer Priaulx Rainier.

She enlarged the outhouse into a spacious workshop for stone and marble carving and used the greenhouse for making plaster casts for bronze, often working outside in the open air. The terraced garden was designed with help from her friend, composer Priaulx Rainier, layered with pathways, trees, ferns, yuccas and a collection of cacti.

In 1968, Barbara Hepworth was recognised for her contribution to British modern art as a 'Dame', though in 1975, a tragic fire at Trewyn Studio led to her death. Following her wishes, the house and studio was opened as the Barbara Hepworth Museum and Sculpture Garden the year after, preserving her atmosphere of creation with tools and materials in place, and a collection of her sculptures. Her work can be seen in the landscape that inspired her at the Yorkshire Sculpture Park, founded in 1977, and at the Hepworth Wakefield, a modern and contemporary art gallery in her birth-town designed by architect David Chipperfield, opened in her honour in 2011.

ABOVE
A painting studio in the house.

RIGHT
A mosaic at the entrance.

OVERLEAF
The exterior of High Sunderland.

26 Bernat Klein | Peter Womersley

Selkirk, Scottish Borders, Scotland

This modular house was a total work of Modern art, design and architecture, functioning as a living, dimensional portfolio for its owner.

Serbian-born textile designer and artist Bernat Klein (1922–2014) established his home and studio in the Scottish Borders – two separate, remarkable Modernist buildings by English architect Peter Womersley (1923–1993). The house of 1958 was the architect's first design for a formal client, and the studio of 1972 was his penultimate built project. While distinct in character, they both framed Klein's work like dimensional portfolios of colour, light and nature.

Klein arrived in Britain in 1945 after studying at the Bauhaus-inspired Bezalel School of Arts and Crafts in Jerusalem. He escaped the Holocaust, though his mother and other members of his Orthodox Jewish family did not. On arrival, he studied textile technology in Leeds, then worked for a knitwear company in Edinburgh and the Scottish Borders. He founded his own company, Colourcraft, in Galashiels in 1952. By the 1960s and 70s, his innovative, rhythmic and colourful woven and screen-printed textiles were attracting leading fashion houses such as Chanel, Dior and Yves Saint Laurent, and British and Scandinavian modern homeware brands.

After seeing the house architect Womersley had built for his own brother (Farnley Hey), Klein commissioned a house from the architect, which became known as 'High Sunderland'. Settled in sloped woodland, the house is built of wood and glass (transparent and coloured), with similarities to the lightweight structures of architect Mies van der Rohe. The modular construction forms an open-plan grid, divided by stepped travertine floor levels and storage integrated into the hardwood walls.

Furniture was upholstered in Klein's own textiles and his vibrant abstract paintings decorated the walls – making it a complete work of architecture, design and art. Klein lived at the house with his family and often entertained clients and hosted events there.

Womersley then designed the artist's studio later in his career; the pair had developed a close friendship after spending most Sundays together at High Sunderland. Womersley connected the house to the Brutalist concrete studio by a path through the

woods, which crossed an entrance bridge to a first-floor entrance. The upper level – for painting, designing and production – was open-plan and wrapped with a continuous ribbon of windows. The ground floor, where visiting clients would enter, was a reception and office.

Whereas High Sunderland almost disappears into the landscape, the studio, with its heavy, horizontal layers, boldly stands out. Today, the house is preserved and privately owned, while the studio, which suffered deterioration over the years, was bought and saved in 2025 by a group including the Bernat Klein Foundation.

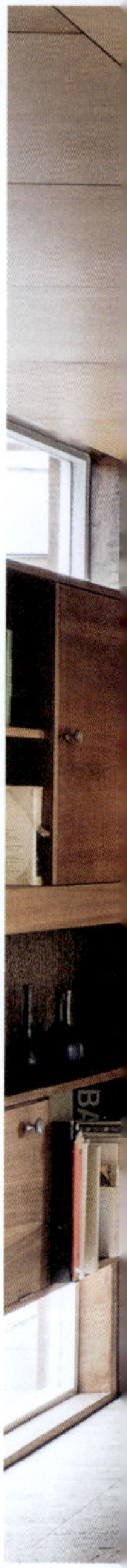

LEFT AND OPPOSITE
The travertine and wood interior scheme.

Furniture was upholstered in Klein's own textiles and his vibrant abstract paintings decorated the walls.

27

Ioanna Veropoulou-Spiteri and Tonis Spiteris | Aristomenes Provelengios

Athens, Greece

This urban house and studio for a sculptor/art-critic couple was designed by a Greek disciple of Le Corbusier and is owned by an architect today.

In the 1950s, Greek sculptor Ioanna Veropoulou-Spiteri (1920–2000) and her husband Tonis Spiteris (1910–1986), an art critic, commissioned a studio in the courtyard of their 1920s home in Athens. They turned to Greek Modern architect Aristomenes Provelengios (1914–1999) who had just returned from ten years' working for Le Corbusier in Paris.

The studio is a compact stack with a dimensional geometric facade of transparent and frosted windows framed in white marble: Modern, yet artisanal in quality. Though it is relatively narrow, inside the spatial quality is generous. By day, Veropoulou-Spiteri's ground-floor double-height studio was illuminated with light, and by night it became a lantern. The lower glass doors slide away to open fully up to the street – ideal for moving large sculptures in and out.

In the studio, Veropoulou-Spiteri's worked on her Cubist sculptures in bronze, marble and wood, influenced by her time living in Paris. Her husband Tonis, who she married in 1941, worked from the mezzanine office space, which sits inside the double-height space like a frame within a frame. He was a writer who interviewed Modern artists such as Lucio Fontana, Salvador Dalí and Constantin Brancusi, and commissioned artists for the Greek pavilion at the Venice Biennale.

Above the staircase, a long trapdoor separates the studio from the living spaces on the third floor. A bedroom and terrace occupy the top floor. The couple travelled for long periods of time, living between Athens, Venice and Paris. While away, they rented the studio to other Modern artists such as Thanasis Tsigos and Dioxandi. Architect Provelengios also lived and worked there for a period of time, designing, painting, writing poetry and teaching.

Today, another Greek architect lives and works in the studio: Dionisis Sotovikis bought the building in 2007 when it was at risk of demolition. He restored it, preserving all original elements and returning it to the original colour scheme. Now it is heritage-protected and living in the house inspires his work every day.

OPPOSITE
The facade of the Spiteris House.

28 Irma Salo Jæger | Irene Sævik

Drøbak, Norway

This 1960s summer cabin was once a peaceful refuge for an abstract artist, today it's a contemporary house inspired by its Modernist origins.

On a tranquil green peninsula overlooking the Oslofjord, the black timber summer cabin of Finnish-Norwegian artist Irma Salo Jæger (b. 1928) was an easy escape from the city, located just an hour away. She went there to immerse in nature and spend time with her husband Tyco Jæger and friends, some of whom also built summer houses close by.

The modest two-bedroom retreat of around 40m² (430ft²) was designed by local architect Hans Grinde in the 1960s. Inspired by the simplicity of Japanese design, rooms had large floor-to-ceiling windows and sliding doors framing views of the forest and the Oslofjord, while the cosy living room had an open fireplace.

The cabin was built in the same decade that Salo Jæger began her career as an artist. She had studied art history in Helsinki, Finland, before moving to Norway to study art in Oslo, where she began experimenting with mixes of oil paint and tempera to achieve a brilliant luminosity in her paintings. Fascinated by colour theory, Op Art and the shifting seasonal effects of light and colour, she originally worked in earthy colours, before amplifying up into bright, energetic compositions often at a large scale. She joined a community of Modern artists including Jakob Weidemann, Johs Rian and Gunnar S. Gundersen who were pioneering abstraction in Norway.

Salo Jæger later explored more dimensionality with kinetic sculptures of aluminium, plastic and light that transformed the rooms around them. Interested in social and environmental issues, she also entered the urban space with public artworks: at Rikshospitalet, the University of Agder, and Bøler metro station in Oslo.

OPPOSITE
The overhanging roof shelters an outdoor corridor.

The new design maintains the original cabin's sense of intimacy through the ever-present experience of the outdoors.

It was in 2003, that architect Irene Sævik bought the cabin. She originally had met Salo Jæger while she was a visiting student at the Oslo Academy of Fine Art. Inspired by the artist's original vision, she decided to extend and renovate the cabin into a house. She added more bedrooms, an office and a sauna within a series of connected pavilions linked by an open-air cloister and a large terrace informed by traditional Norwegian vernacular structures.

One section of Sævik's roof cantilevers out over the rocks, deepening the connection of the house to the landscape and creating a natural ladder up to the roof deck. The new design maintains the original cabin's sense of intimacy through its warm timber-panelled walls and the ever-present experience of the outdoors. Sævik invited Salo Jæger back to the house to visit after it was finished.

ABOVE
The cosy wood-panelled living room.

OPPOSITE
The contemporary black timber house in nature.

29

Sigurjón Ólafsson | Skarphéðinn Jóhannsson

Reykjavík, Iceland

The sculptor found his workshop and family home in a former military barracks, which was transformed in the 1960s with a Modern design.

Icelandic artist Sigurjón Ólafsson (1908–1982) adapted a former military barracks by the sea in Reykjavík into his home and studio in the 1940s: it was a life of pure economy, where art was the priority. In the 1960s, fellow Modernist, Icelandic architect Skarphéðinn Jóhannsson, designed him a new workshop and extended the house.

Ólafsson trained as a house painter, before studying art in Denmark from 1928 and establishing a successful career as a Modern artist there, with his monumental, organic sculptures of clay, wood, stone and concrete that blended Abstraction and Realism. His work inspired Danish designer Finn Juhl, who designed a house for the sculptor and his first wife Tove Ólafsson in Denmark.

Yet in 1945, he returned to Iceland homesick and settled in Reykjavík, adapting a corrugated-steel Nissen hut into his workshop. The small stone officer's house next door became his home where he lived with his second wife Inga Birgitta Spur, who he married in 1956.

In 1961, architect Jóhannsson – who studied in Copenhagen and worked under Kaare Klint and Alvar Aalto – designed a single-storey wooden extension to the stone house with large picture windows to the sea. It was simple, yet Spur brought a warm touch to the functional house for the family of six, which was lined with Siberian pine and became an overflow store for Ólafsson's sculptures.

There were so many sculptures in the workshop – including his popular modelled portrait busts, which supported his abstract practice – that Jóhannsson had to build the new studio on top of the old one, constructing a spacious timber hall with simple triangular buttresses and clerestory windows to ensure privacy and good light all day. The wooden slats were finished with black-brown-coloured tar oil, a traditional vernacular finish, that ensured waterproofing and low maintenance.

OPPOSITE
The wood-panelled interior of the house.

Siberian pine clads the interior of the house, which became an overflow store for Ólafsson's sculptures.

In 1984, two years after Sigurjón Ólafsson passed away, Spur commissioned the architect son of Jóhannsson, Ögmundur, to convert the workshop and the stone house into a museum dedicated to Ólafsson's legacy. Among other updates, a second level was added to the stone house and the workshop was painted white, so it now stands out in the landscape as a modern, geometric volume.

The museum opened in 1988 and exhibits sculptures, alone or in dialogue with other artists, alongside an archive, research centre and cafe. Spur lives in the black wooden house, surrounded by sculptures. In 2012, the Sigurjón Ólafsson Museum was donated to the Icelandic state and became a division of the National Gallery of Iceland, and it is currently managed by the family, including Spur.

ABOVE
The white-painted Modern workshop, now a museum.

In the 1980s the workshop was painted white, so it now stands out in the landscape as a modern, geometric volume.

The House in Modern Art

How did artists depict and interrogate the idea of the house in art during the 20th century? The house as a symbol, subject, concept and object.

The house went on an epic journey in the 20th century. War and displacement tore artists away from their homes; Modern women artists challenged the conventions and gender roles of the home; and urbanisation in cities such as New York and Tokyo saw the single-family house becoming less relevant as a subject.

Artists have been depicting houses in paintings over centuries, yet in the 20th century they began making sculptures of houses, building houses in galleries, destroying houses, carving houses into their skin: the house emerged in new forms of expression as a metaphor for false stability, domestic prisons and broken promises.

After all, artists are critical thinkers who magnify the cracks in society. With shifts to social dynamics – from queer relationships, feminism and divorce, to civil rights, the growth of the middle classes and the AIDS epidemic – artists were questioning the values that the single-family house had been built upon, and the initial optimism of modern architecture.

The house as symbol

Nevertheless, the house remains an enduring symbol for shelter, safety, comfort, privacy, autonomy, sanctuary and creativity – all

Arakawa and Gins, *Drawing for Container of Perceiving*, 1984

the more powerful in precarious times. In our singular domestic paradises, life feels controllable, time slows, we can feel like ourselves and be closest to the people we love: the architectural form of the house itself is a universal symbol for this feeling.

The modern painters of the late 19th and early 20th century truly captured this feeling on their canvases: see Gabriele Münter's yellow house in Bavaria that she shared with Wassily Kandinsky or Claude Monet's pink house with its water lilies and Japanese bridge in Giverny. While painted in the same style, Edvard Munch's blood-red house depicted in the painting 'Red Virginia Creeper' appears to be both melting and burning – it's unsettlingly foreboding.

The Surrealists liked both the effect of melting and the symbol of the house. For them, the house was a metaphor of the self and the status quo. Their Surrealist manifesto published in 1925 states: 'We have no intention of changing man's habits, but we have hopes of proving to them how fragile their thoughts are, and on what unstable foundations, over what cellars they have erected their unsteady houses.' (1)

Artist Christopher Wood painted a zebra in front of Le Corbusier's renowned Villa Savoye in 'Zebra and Parachute' (1930). Dorothea Tanning's painting 'On Time Off Time' (1948) shows the timber foundation of a house accompanied by flames, smoke and a floating sunflower, echoing the cabin she and Max Ernst built in the Arizona desert after fleeing war in Europe.

Reclaiming and rebuilding the house

For women artists, the house was a site of reinvention in the 20th century. In Europe, modernity brought with it domestic conveniences such as washing machines and fridges – speeding up the mundane everyday tasks expected of daughters and wives. Gradually the social freedom of women began to grow, starting with wealthy women who began to be admitted into art school from the late 19th century.

'What makes modernism modern is the participation of women artists, and the freedom with which they could paint,' writes art historian Katy Hessel, in *The Story of Art without Men* (2022). (2) She highlights a painting by Gwen John, an artist who earned her own keep in Paris in the early 20th century, titled 'A corner of an artist's room in Paris' (1907): 'It signifies her freedom,' Hessel reflects – precisely because it was not a house with domestic responsibility and a family. (3)

While the Bauhaus promoted equality between genders, its director Walter Gropius held the belief that men thought in three dimensions while women were limited to two. Gertrud Arndt joined the Bauhaus to study architecture, yet found it hostile and took up photography instead. (4) Sophie Taeuber-Arp, who designed and built her own house, had to balance two personas at her own dinner table as intellectual artist and wife hostess (see entry 2). (5)

Many of the women artists in this book bravely rejected conventions and lived their lives unapologetically with freedom: Tamara de Lempicka, a divorced woman active on the Paris social scene of the 1920s; Amaza Lee Meredith, who had a female life partner; Ruth Asawa, who balanced and blended family life with six children while working from home as an artist (see entries 8, 37 and 44). Their houses did not follow preconceived gender expectations of the single-family house, but reflected their own identities instead.

The symbol of the traditional house became a tool for feminist expression, subverted and reframed. Faith Ringgold worked with female inmates at the Correctional Institute for Women on Rikers Island to create the mural 'For the Women's House' (1971), depicting interracial women in diverse professional roles. In 1972, 'Womanhouse', curated by Judy Chicago and Miriam Schapiro in California, brought together artists and students to critique the domestic roles of women within the rooms of a dilapidated house. Modern women artists broke down the walls that suffocated them and rebuilt the house as their own.

Elimination of the house

Abstract painting of the 20th century in all its forms – from De Stijl to Abstract Expressionism – boldly eliminated subjects in preference of geometry or expression. Even if a painting was titled 'house', it often didn't look like a house – it was the artist's emotional or imaginative visual response to that subject – leaving the viewer to read between the lines: when subjects provided no structure, it was up to the viewer to build it.

The psychological impact of architectural and urban destruction in World War II, for example in Hiroshima, also contributed to the deconstruction of the house in art. Belgian artist Léon Wuidar's (see entry 23) geometric paintings were the product of his childhood surrounded by the construction waste of post-war Belgium. Art critic Laura Cumming reads between the lines, detecting: 'A secret passage, a bunker, a side view into a dead end, the place in a house where a person might hide'. (6)

In the second half of the century, in cities the concepts of privacy and ownership associated with the house began to break down with high-rise apartment living, to a background of urban 'renewal' that left cities as construction sites and mentally exhausting places to live in, an era that to some extent we still exist in today. Consequently, artists began to express the dissolution and violent destruction of the house.

Fluxus artist Alison Knowles' 'House of Dust' (1967) dissolved the house into a computerised poem, reducing it to a randomised and impersonal automated sum of its parts: material, site, inhabitants. In the 1970s, Gordon Matta-Clark was slicing up suburban houses with chainsaws and shooting out windows with airguns in Harlem, while Louise Nevelson was constructing dystopian walls from demolition waste in Manhattan. In 1990s London, Rachel Whiteread used a Victorian terraced house as a cast for concrete, receiving an audience of more than 100,000 before it was ceremoniously demolished to make way for the development of housing towers.

The rise of the modern city

In place of the house, the modern city in all its facets emerged as a new subject matter. Post-war modern cities were urbanising at an accelerating rate, increasing in complexity – casting new shadows, forging connections, reducing distances, social spaces, perspectives and viewpoints.

In Rome in 1909, Futurist artist Giacomo Balla painted a street light, translating the dazzling new illumination of the city at night. In 1920s New York, Georgia O'Keeffe painted skyscrapers from the street and the views over the East River from her room at the high-rise Shelton Hotel on Lexington Avenue: 'I realize it's unusual for an artist to want to work way up near the roof of a big hotel in the heart of the roaring city but I think that's just what the artist of today needs for stimulus,' she wrote in 1928 (7) – although it was in the antithetical deserted landscapes of New Mexico where she built her house and found lifelong inspiration.

After World War II, Tokyo was dramatically and rapidly urbanising with towering concrete buildings. Architect Kazuo Shinohara (see entry 32) argued in his essay 'The house is art' that the house had become 'a small bubble in contemporary building production' overtaken in importance by mass housing, transport and infrastructure. The house had become more of a conceptual art form for architects to work on, less relevant as a functional structure and more as a place of experimentation. (8) This came to be in the work of Arakawa and Gins (see entry 39), who saw the house as a place to challenge ourselves beyond our comfort zone, rather than creating one.

Commodification of the house

The house was reborn as a consumer symbol at the end of the century. Post-war social housing was becoming privatised thanks to new access to credit, the introduction of the standardised mortgage in the US and Margaret Thatcher's 'Right to Buy' scheme introduced in 1979 in the UK. Capitalist governments encouraged home ownership through political policy and houses became desirable, aspirational objects, locking owners into debt which encouraged them to work harder. The consumerist domestic lifestyle was promoted alongside the house.

Laurie Simmons' 'Walking House' (1989) depicted the slim legs of a woman beneath an American suburban dream house: 'We live in a blazingly consumer-oriented society, where the things around us control us, and I think these images are about the way a person can be subsumed by what's around them,' she explained. (9)

Catherine Opie's 'Self-Portrait/Cutting' (1993) photographic self-portrait depicts a child's drawing of two women holding hands in front of a house – carved into the bleeding skin of her back. For the queer artist during the AIDS crisis it signified her unattainable yearning for domestic bliss, a mould that she did not fit into and felt was out of reach. She went on to photograph the facades of Beverly Hills mansions exploring ideas of wealth, privacy and social exclusion.

Confirming the house as an object was Roy Lichtenstein's glorification of it in his 'House' series of sculptures in the 1990s. These sculptures appear to be dimensional, yet are like flat billboards made of aluminium: their thin construction represented how flimsy their values had become. Despite its persistent associations with permanence and solidity, the house has been on a wild ride, and this essay is merely one reading of the ride, scratching the surface of the ideas, concepts and symbolic nature of the house in the 20th century which is varied, multifaceted and distinct across movements, cultures and geographies.

倉彫塑館

30

Fumio Asakura

Tokyo, Japan

The sculptor's traditional Japanese house and radical studio building in Tokyo mark the meeting of East and West, and the two sides of his sensibility.

From the 1930s, Japanese sculptor Fumio Asakura (1883–1964) designed his own home and studio in the historic Yanaka neighbourhood of Tokyo. Just like his sculptures, his architectural concept fused ideas from East and West: a traditional Japanese wooden courtyard house, connected to a bold, raw, concrete studio that experimented with the latest construction techniques.

Born in a small village in western Kyushu, Asakura moved to Tokyo at the age of 19 to study at the Tokyo School of Fine Arts, graduating in 1907. He went on to pioneer Modern Western-style sculpture in Japan, influenced by the bronze figures of Auguste Rodin (1840–1917). His smooth, realist sculptures lyrically captured everyday people, as well as the sinuous forms of local cats.

He first designed the two-storey Japanese house to live in with his family, set around a tranquil courtyard with a natural pond, plum trees and ferns. In 1936 he added the three-storey modern studio – an asymmetric group of concrete blocks with curved edges and textured surfaces painted black to the street, and white towards the courtyard.

Inside the studio building, where he opened a sculpture school, high ceilings and large skylights created a dynamic experience of space, very different in character from the intimacy of the traditional house. The second floor had a greenhouse for orchids and there was a tearoom on the third floor, for meetings with visitors and friends. In the rooftop garden planted with Western flowers and plants including roses, tulips and old olive trees, there are two sculptures by Asakura – a cement bust of Langdon Warner, the American art historian who specialised in East Asian Art, and the young 'Shotputter' who watches over the low-rise neighbourhood.

Asakura passed away in 1964, after making an impression on generations of artists as a teacher and mentor at the University of Tokyo. His home and studio opened as the Asakura Museum of Sculpture in 1967 and were recognised on the register of National Tangible Cultural Property in 2001.

OPPOSITE
The black concrete exterior of the studio.

31

Isamu Noguchi

Long Island City, New York, US; Mure, Japan

In New York and Japan, the artist built two transcendental complexes where sculpture, architecture, environment and life are inseparable.

The sculptures, furniture, lighting and landscapes of Japanese American artist Isamu Noguchi (1904–1988) are grounded in his sensitive approach to Modernism informed by nature, craft and humanity. At the height of his career in the 1960s he established two self-designed studios – the first in Long Island City, New York, and the second in Mure, Japan.

Born to a Japanese father and American mother in Los Angeles, Noguchi grew up between the two countries. He apprenticed in the US under sculptor of Mount Rushmore, Gutzon Borglum, and then in Paris with Constantin Brancusi.

He went on to collaborate with leading figures of the Modern movement including Buckminster Fuller, Diego Rivera and furniture manufacturers Herman Miller and Hans Knoll. After World War II, during which he was interned in a Japanese-American prison camp, his work expanded into designs for playgrounds, plazas and gardens.

In 1961, Noguchi moved his studio from bustling Greenwich Village to a warehouse in the relatively remote Long Island City in Queens. In 1974, he expanded into a red-brick building opposite, and then an adjacent gas station creating an open-air gallery within the industrial architecture.

From 1961, he set up a studio complex in Mure on the island of Shikoku, known for its granite stonemasonry. He worked with architect Tadashi Yamamoto and stone-cutter Masatoshi Izumi over a period of 20 years to develop houses, workshops and a sculpture garden. They rebuilt an Edo-period merchant's home for Noguchi, and in 1972 a rough-hewn stone house for Izumi with a red structural truss system, fusing high-tech construction with low-tech local vernacular.

Today, both places are open to the public to visit as the Noguchi Museum in New York and the Isamu Noguchi Garden Museum in Japan.

ABOVE
Isamu Noguchi's sculptures at his studio in Mure, Japan.

32

Kiyoji Otsuji | Kazuo Shinohara

Tokyo, Japan

Mirroring the concrete infrastructure of the modern city, the House in Uehara speculated upon a new type of metaphysical domestic architecture.

Japanese photographer Kiyoji Otsuji (1923–2001) commissioned a family house with a darkroom and studio from architect Kazuo Shinohara (1925–2006) in the 1970s. Located in the bustling Tokyo district of Shibuya, the 'House in Uehara' was the first concrete house in the neighbourhood, commanding attention with its enigmatic architecture that straddled Brutalist sculpture and urban infrastructure.

Otsuji studied photography in Tokyo in the early 1940s and became a renowned photographer, writer and teacher on the post-war avant-garde scene. In the 1950s, he co-founded the photography and design studio Graphic Group and participated in the artists collective Jikken Kobo (Experimental Workshop).

In the early 1960s, Otsuji asked architect Shinohara to design him a countryside summer house: the 'House with an Earthen Floor' was a low-tech, one-storey structure with a traditional pitched roof, built of wood and paper screens informed by the local vernacular. When it came to their second, later collaboration, the 'House in Uehara' completed in 1976, the urban design was a stark contrast.

The hefty concrete box with triangular windows is topped with a semi-circular 'hat' with round windows. The form aligns in weight and scale to a piece of urban infrastructure such as a bridge, rather than that of a single-family house. Inside, the exposed concrete structure of six columns with Y-shaped branches is a constant presence to everyday activities. Like a Brutalist tree-house, it interrogates the tension between irregular natural geometries and the complexity of urban life.

OPPOSITE
The concrete structure in the living room.

Shinohara disrupted all preceding design hierarchies and embraced the aesthetic language of technology, science and machines.

The studio was on the ground floor and the bedrooms located on the first and third floors. On the second floor the living area includes a kitchen and dining space with a long table and two long benches either side. This became a gathering place for family, friends, collaborators and students to meet, lit throughout the day by a skylight above.

Architect Shinohara studied in Tokyo and became a professor and philosopher, deeply contemplating the new concrete landscape of the modern city. While his early work embraced vernacular (as seen at the 'House with an Earthen Floor'), from the 1970s he began to interpret the visual urban chaos of Tokyo through his architecture. He disrupted all preceding design hierarchies and embraced the aesthetic language of technology, science and machines.

Otsuji gave Shinohara total freedom in his design for the 'House in Uehara', which influenced a later generation of architects including Toyo Ito and Itsuko Hasegawa who became known as the 'Shinohara school'. Today Otsuji's family lives in the Tokyo house and still spend summers at the 'House with an Earthen Floor'.

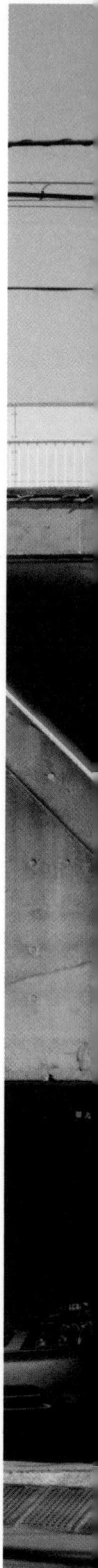

OPPOSITE
The House in Uehara.

33

Demas Nwoko

Ibadan, Nigeria

This Tropical Modern house and studio became a hive for artistic collaboration across all mediums, fusing 20th-century ideas with traditional culture.

Working across art, theatre, architecture, construction and craft, Demas Nwoko (b. 1935) explores the tension, balance and beauty of the dialogue between eurocentric Modernism and African cultural traditions and vernacular. He innovated a Tropical Modern architectural style in Nigeria that promoted functionalist living, while employing local building materials and reliable localised approaches adapted to the humid and rainy climate.

Nwoko studied art at Nigeria's College of Art, Science and Technology in Zaria, where he co-founded the Zaria Art Society, which debated how eurocentric and African artistic approaches should be combined. After a scholarship in Paris, in 1962 he began lecturing in drama at the University of Ibadan in Nigeria where he was a key player in the Mbari Writers and Artists Club, shaping modern Nigerian expression after independence in 1960.

In 1967, Nwoko began building the ever-evolving 'New Culture Studio' in Ibadan, a hub for collaborative projects across theatre, architecture and publishing. It began as a three-storey home and sculpture studio, then expanded into a cultural centre with another larger two-storey building, wood workshop and semi-circular amphitheatre built of local granite stone.

The design used vernacular building materials, combined with modern construction technology. Laterite earth was mixed with Portland cement to make strong blocks, while interiors were clad with appa wood. Integrated furniture was made of southern Nigerian hardwoods and the concrete staircase clad in black granite. A sculptural *ezi-ubulu* collects rainwater through a square oculus into a shallow blue-tiled pool, while louvred windows and a ventilation stack encourage the flow of cool air.

Since 1977, Nwoko has lived at his home and studio in Idumuje-Ugboko, a brick building with a pointed, overhanging roof that shades a porch. Here he expanded ideas established in Ibadan, with a sculptural fibreglass *ezi-ubulu*, passive ventilation system and laterite block construction. Today, his family continue the work of the New Culture Studios, Nwoko's vibrant complex that unites architecture, traditional culture and modernity.

OPPOSITE
The ezi-ubulu at the New Culture Studio house.

NEXT PAGE
The New Culture Studio.

34

Jacques Majorelle | Paul Sinoir

Marrakech, Morocco

Art Deco meets Moroccan craft at the vivid blue Villa Dar Saada, a sanctuary for artists over generations surrounded by a verdant botanic garden.

This villa at the heart of the Jardins Majorelle botanic garden in Marrakech has two 20th-century chapters. The first, as a painting studio for French artist Jacques Majorelle (1886–1962) from the 1930s, while the second is that of Yves Saint Laurent and Pierre Bergé, the cosmopolitan couple who converted the villa into the Museum of Berber Arts.

Born in Nancy, painter Majorelle was the son of a French Art Nouveau furniture designer. After studying art in Paris, he began travelling to Morocco which was under French colonial rule from 1912–56. In 1923, he commissioned the traditional Villa Bou Saf Saf and in the 1930s asked Parisian architect Paul Sinoir to add an adjacent modern painting studio, which became known as the Villa Dar Saada.

Composed of a collection of stacked cubes with flat roofs, the studio was a modern contrast to the main villa. Its terraces have curved tubular steel railings in the Art Deco style and patterned Moroccan tiled floors inside. Originally painted white, it was later painted in the breathtaking 'Majorelle Blue'.

Majorelle lived in the Villa Bou Saf Saf, painted in the Villa Dar Saada and opened his impressive surrounding botanic garden to the public in the 1940s. He inhabited this artistic paradise until 1962, when he returned to France due to health issues and unfortunately never returned.

In 1974, French fashion designer Saint Laurent and his partner, industrialist Bergé, bought the Villa Bou Saf Saf, which they renamed Villa Oasis. It became an eccentric sanctuary with chandeliers, leopard-print sofas and guests such as Andy Warhol. In the 1980s they bought the garden and the Villa Dar Saada too, reviving the original spirit of the place with the help of garden designer Madison Cox.

The Fondation Jardin Majorelle was established in 2001 to manage the gardens and villas. The Villa Dar Saada now exhibits Saint Laurent and Bergé's collection of cultural objects of the Indigenous Berbers of North Africa, and the Yves Saint Laurent Museum designed by French architects Studio KO opened in 2017.

OPPOSITE
The 'Majorelle Blue' facade of the Villa Dar Saada.

35

Ena de Silva | Geoffrey Bawa

Colombo, Sri Lanka

Reclaiming tradition with a Modernist twist, this tropical urban house echoed the artistic approach of its owner and is now part of a rural hotel.

Designing the house of artist Ena de Silva (1922–2015) in Colombo in 1962 was a turning point in the career of architect Geoffrey Bawa (1919–2003). Collaborative conversations between artist and architect resulted in a novel fusion of Modernism with the local Kandyan style, a Tropical Modern synthesis that Bawa became renowned for.

The house was formed of a sprawling set of white cubed volumes with traditional terracotta tiled roofs, which were connected by shaded loggias and planted courtyards. Sculptural concrete staircases twisted through cool, airy open walled rooms with wooden shutters instead of glass windows.

It was a calming living environment for Sri Lankan-born de Silva, who reinvigorated the ancient batik fabric patterning technique with modern motifs and formats. The craft had been suppressed from the late 19th century thanks to industrial-scale Dutch imitations, yet independence from British colonial rule in Sri Lanka emboldened her reclaiming of the tradition.

Before designing de Silva's house, Bawa had been transforming a former rubber estate known as Lunuganga into a tropical garden influenced by the Italian Renaissance. He then decided to study architecture at the Architectural Association in London, returning to Sri Lanka in the late 1950s with a new modern outlook.

After de Silva's house, he designed further houses, hotels and the Sri Lankan Parliament building, working with collaborators including de Silva, Danish architect Ulrik Plesner, Tamil engineer K Poologasundram, designer Barbara Sansoni and Laki Senanayake.

De Silva moved out of the house in the mid-1970s, Bawa established an office there and it then became home to Belgian painter Saskia Pintelon for 22 years. When threatened by demolition, the Geoffrey Bawa Trust dismantled and relocated the entire house to the Lunuganga estate, completing the process in 2016. It now hosts guests as part of a hotel that honours the legacy of Bawa and de Silva.

OPPOSITE
The white exterior of the house.

OVERLEAF
A courtyard and open-air room of the house.

36

Sydney Ball and Lynne Eastaway | Glenn Murcutt

Glenorie, New South Wales, Australia

Suspended in the landscape, this remote house designed for an artist couple fuses Modernism with environmentalism.

In a wild forest north of Sydney, this retreat for an artist couple – Sydney Ball (1933–2017) and Lynne Eastaway (b. 1949) – was designed in 1977 by architect Glenn Murcutt (b. 1936). It was carefully engineered to preserve its immediate environmental eco-system, resting on stilts above the land with a passive cooling system.

Artists Ball and Eastaway met in the early 1970s when Eastaway enrolled at the National Art School in Sydney where Ball was then teaching. After studying in New York City, Ball had developed a bold, geometric artistic style informed by Abstract Expressionism. Eastaway's paintings were equally as vibrant and, after graduating, she also began teaching art in Sydney.

Their house – a private escape from the city – is totally immersed in nature and features a lightweight steel structure supported by 14 stilts that rest inside 14 holes on a sandstone ledge. The arched corrugated sheet-metal roof is carved with skylights and opens up at each end to outdoor decks. It's all bolted and screwed together for disassembly without trace and has a rainwater recycling system and sprinkler system for fire protection.

Murcutt had only established his studio in Sydney a few years earlier in 1969, yet was already renowned for his modern sustainable approach. Born in London, he grew up in New Guinea where his self-sufficient father, a carpenter, had designed a house on stilts in corrugated iron. With the threat of Japanese invasion, the family moved to Australia in 1941 and Murcutt studied architecture in Sydney before travelling in Europe where he was inspired by the sensitive Modernism of Finnish architect Alvar Aalto.

Though Eastaway and Ball separated, they remained close. Deeply informed by the historic culture of the Australian bush, Ball lived at the house until his death in 2017. After some time, Eastaway returned and her paintings evolved with the seasonal colours of the forest.

OPPOSITE
The open-plan living space.

OVERLEAF
The Ball-Eastaway House.

37

Amaza Lee Meredith

Virginia, US

Azurest South was the ground-breaking International Style home of a progressive academic couple who surpassed aesthetic and social conventions.

Black artist, academic and architect Amaza Lee Meredith (1895–1984) designed this house known as 'Azurest South' in 1938 for herself and her life partner Dr Edna Meade Colson, an educator and community activist. Influenced by Bauhaus style Modernism, it broke new ground as the first 'International Style' building of its kind in the area.

Meredith was born in Lynchburg to a white carpenter father and a Black seamstress mother, who were prohibited from marrying due to segregation laws. Her father built their family home and she absorbed the architectural process from design to construction, yet could not study architecture due to her race and gender.

Instead, she trained as a teacher, specialising in art at Virginia State College, where she met Colson in 1915, an educated, upper-middle-class teacher, descended from free African Americans. To reach degree level, Meredith had to travel north to New York City where in 1925 she studied art at Columbia Teachers College under Arthur Wesley Dow, later returning for her Masters in art education.

There, she absorbed Modernist aesthetics at MoMA's seminal 1932 'Modern Architecture: International Exhibition' and through the cultural movement of the Harlem Renaissance, which celebrated Black heritage and culture. Equipped with confidence, she returned to establish the Department of Art at Virginia State College, where she developed a curriculum exploring topics such as African aesthetics, photography and graphic design – showing students how art could be employed in industries such as advertising and appreciated for self-discovery.

Influenced by Bauhaus style Modernism, Azurest South broke new ground as the first 'International Style' building in the area.

ABOVE
The entrance of the house.

Meredith designed Azurest South on a green plot of land, adjacent to the campus of Virginia State University. The flat-roofed, single-storey house is clad in white stucco and its asymmetrical massing of blocks shows hints of Art Deco with curving edges, bands of glass blocks and a turquoise trim. Part house, part studio, the interior design was informed by colour theory, with chrome and black lacquer finishes.

She went on to design many houses for her friends and family, as well as establishing 'Azurest North' in Sag Harbor, New York, with her sister Maude Terry. The holiday resort of modern flat-roofed cottages with colourful cabin-like interiors became a popular retreat for middle-class Black people. Terry Cottage, built in 1940, was Meredith and Colson's own summer house. Azurest South now serves as the Virginia State University Alumni House, and is registered as a landmark and historic place.

38 Marguerite Wildenhain | Albert Lanier

Guerneville, California, US

The Bauhaus ceramic artist settled in rural Northern California at Pond Farm, where rustic vernacular met Modernism.

Bauhaus-trained master potter Marguerite Wildenhain (1896–1985) found refuge in Northern California, where she established her home, studio and ceramics school within a complex of modern timber buildings in a redwood valley. Credited with bringing Modernist European studio ceramics to America, she lived and worked at Pond Farm for nearly forty years.

Born in France, Wildenhain (née Friedlaender) studied sculpture and pottery, before joining the Bauhaus school in Weimar, where she became the first woman to earn the 'Master Potter' status in Germany. Yet, with Jewish heritage and the rise of the Nazis, she fled to the Netherlands and then to the US in 1940.

After teaching at the California College of Arts and Crafts, in 1942, architect Gordon Herr and heiress Jane Herr invited her, alongside other artists, to help establish the Pond Farm Workshops near Guerneville, north of San Francisco. The farm hosted weaving, metal-smithing and mural-painting classes for a few years until it closed. Wildenhain stayed on to establish her own ceramics summer school, where she taught students how to balance precision and improvisation, and emphasised process over results.

At Pond Farm, her simple house was clad in redwood and shingle panels, while a guest house was designed by modern architect Albert Lanier (Ruth Asawa's husband, see entry 44). When not teaching, she developed her own earthy semi-matte vases, teapots and decorative tiles with designs informed by nature and her travels across America.

California State Parks began acquiring land to establish the Austin Creek State Recreation Area in 1963, including the land of Pond Farm Workshops, yet they respected Wildenhain's lease. In 2012, restoration work was carried out to open the workshops to the public and host an artist residency. In 2014, Pond Farm was recognised on the National Register of Historic Places, and in 2023 it was designated a National Historic Landmark.

OPPOSITE
Wildenhain's teaching studio.

39 Arakawa and Gins

East Hampton, US

As Late Modernism gave way to urban monotony, the house designs of this artist duo sought to surprise, stimulate and reactivate the body and senses.

Shusaku Arakawa (1936–2010) and Madeline Gins (1941–2014) joined forces as an artistic duo named Arakawa and Gins from the 1960s until the end of their lives. Through painting, poetry, installations, architecture, philosophy and science, they explored topics connected to the body, mental health and mortality. Their principal theory of 'Reversible Destiny' examined the concept of ageing backwards.

The architectural structures of Arakawa and Gins were a reaction against the mindless monotony and decreased quality of Late Modernist architecture. Operating like a laboratory, the artists designed dysfunctional, inconvenient spaces that awaken inhabitants physically and mentally, rather than boring them. They believed humans were inseparable from the houses they live in.

Born in Japan, Arakawa studied art in Tokyo, where he joined the Neo-Dadaist Organisers, a movement founded in 1960 in the wake of rapid post-war modernisation. New Yorker Gins studied physics and Eastern philosophy, interested in fiction and poetry. Arakawa moved to New York in 1961, befriending conceptual artists such as Marcel Duchamp and composer John Cage, and he met Gins soon after.

Their first project together was a human-sized puzzle testing semiotics and linguistics. Next came an artwork on the pavements of Manhattan, testing perception and consciousness. Without any formal architectural training, in the 1980s they began designing speculative buildings and in the 1990s their sites of 'Reversible Destiny' actually began to materialise: employing undulating floors, unexpected shifts in scale, affronting clashes of colour to stimulate and activate their inhabitants.

In Gifu, Japan, at their perception-shifting 18,000m^2 (194,000ft^2) Yoro Park (1995), a maze unfolds inside the 'Critical Resemblance House'. In 2005 came the 'Reversible Destiny Lofts Mitaka', a wacky apartment complex in Tokyo with nonsensical interiors, dedicated to Helen Keller, the American deafblind disability activist who they admired. Then, in 2008, they built the Bioscleave House (Lifespan Extending Villa) in East Hampton,

ABOVE
The Reversible Destiny Office at Yoro Park.

Arakawa and Gins believed humans were inseparable from the houses they live in.

New York, with its eccentric silhouette and a sand-dune-style interior painted in 52 colours, which was commissioned by Italian art collector Angela Gallmann for Carl Koch, a pioneer of prefab construction.

Arakawa and Gins later expanded their vision to an urban scale with designs for public housing and city plans through drawings, studies and models. In 2010, the year Arakawa passed away, they founded the Reversible Destiny Foundation in New York. Then in 2013, Gins' last project, the Biotopological Scale-Juggling Escalator, was created for Dover Street Market in Manhattan, commissioned by Rei Kawakubo of Comme des Garçons. The Reversible Destiny Lofts in Tokyo welcome visitors for tours and life-extending overnight stays.

OPPOSITE
The interior of the Reversible Destiny Office.

40

Suzy Frelinghuysen and George L K Morris | George Sanderson, John Butler Swann

Lenox, Massachusetts, US

The 1930s studio and 1940s house of an industrious artist couple who collected Modern European art including Picasso, Léger and Matisse.

North of New York City in the leafy Berkshires, two artists, Suzy Frelinghuysen (1911–1988) and George L K Morris (1905–1975), were art collectors, intellectuals and pioneers of Bauhaus Modernism in America. Built in the 1930s and 40s, their white, geometric house and studio with glass block windows is said to be the first Modernist structure in New England.

Born into an affluent family, Morris studied at Yale then travelled to Paris in the 1920s with artist and collector A E Gallatin, his cousin – who founded the Gallery of Living Art in 1927, the first public collection of modern art in America, which predated MoMA by two years. The pair mixed with artists such as Picasso, Braque and Brancusi. Morris studied art in the painting studios of Fernand Léger (see entry 5) and Amédée Ozenfant (see entry 7).

Ozenfant's studio designed by Le Corbusier became the inspiration for Morris's own art studio back home, built in 1930 and designed with assistance from Boston architect George Sanderson, who he met at Yale. It was located on the grounds of his parents' country estate, 'Brookhurst'. Morris returned to Europe throughout the 1930s collecting abstract art.

In 1935, he married New Jersey-born Frelinghuysen, who had studied art and music from a young age and also travelled widely in Europe. The pair were among the founding members of the American Abstract Artists group in 1936. Morris encouraged Frelinghuysen's painting, and in 1938 she became the first woman artist in the collection of what had now been renamed the Museum of Living Art.

In 1941, the couple commissioned local architect John Butler Swann to design their modern house connected to the studio, funded by the sale of a Picasso to art collector Peggy Guggenheim. Swann combined Modernist ideas with his own interest in Indigenous adobe buildings of Arizona and New Mexico. There are floors in local Lee marble and Argentinian

OPPOSITE
The interior of the Frelinghuysen Morris House and Studio.

leather, glass block walls and geometric frescos by Frelinghuysen; modern furniture by Paul Frankl, Gilbert Rohde and Alvar Aalto; and artworks by Picasso, Gris, Matisse and Léger.

After World War II Frelinghuysen began singing lead roles for the New York City Opera, touring Europe and America. She retired in 1951 and pursued painting full time. In the 1950s, Morris's

ABOVE
The white exterior informed by Le Corbusier.

receding checkerboard paintings anticipated Op Art and in the 1960s his artwork gained recognition. He was fatally injured in an automobile accident in 1975. Frelinghuysen died in 1988 and outlined her wish that the house and art collection be shared to further the understanding of abstract art. Today it is open to the public to visit, with original furniture and artworks in place.

41

Willem de Kooning

New York, US

The Abstract Expressionist designed his own timber and steel house and studio in East Hampton in the 1960s.

Dutch-born artist Willem de Kooning (1904–1997) arrived in New York in the mid-1920s and became known for his vivid, energetic paintings in the Abstract Expressionist style. In the 1960s, at a high point in his career, he became a US citizen and built a modern house and studio in East Hampton.

The artist grew up in a working-class family in Rotterdam, where at just 12 years old he apprenticed at a design firm and shortly after began evening classes in art at what is now the Willem de Kooning Academie. In 1926, he stowed away on a ship to the US, where in Jazz Age New York he worked under Fernand Léger (see entry 5) at the public mural division of the Works Progress Administration. He found success in the late 1940s alongside artists such as Jackson Pollock, Barnett Newman and Mark Rothko.

The power of Abstract Expressionism saw the centre of Modern art shift from Paris to New York, yet in 1963, de Kooning stepped back from the potent pace of Manhattan, first partly and then fully relocating to a quiet, leafy neighbourhood in East Hampton. There he designed a light-filled, open-plan timber house and studio, which was both rural and high-tech in identity, with an exposed white-painted steel structure and a V-shaped 'butterfly roof'.

In the airy studio, wooden benches doubled up as storage, and a pulley hoisted and rotated the easel to shift its perspectives. Here, de Kooning began adding safflower cooking oil to his paint to make it more slippery, expressing a new looseness and softness informed by the trees and the beach.

The 1970s brought more experimentation, yet his health declined in the 1980s and he painted his last work in 1991. De Kooning's home and studio has been preserved by his family. Close by in East Hampton is the former mid-century house of his wife, fellow Abstract Expressionist Elaine de Kooning (now an artists' residency), as well as the house and studio of artists Jackson Pollock and Lee Krasner.

OPPOSITE
Willem de Kooning's East Hampton house.

The walls were opened up with huge picture windows and skylights brought in more natural light from above.

OPPOSITE
The modernised Pueblo style house.

42

Georgia O'Keeffe

New Mexico, US

With help from her friend Maria Chabot, the artist modernised an old adobe Pueblo style house in Abiquiú, which today is her house museum.

The diverse landscapes of New Mexico were a source of eternal inspiration, solitude and freedom for American artist Georgia O'Keeffe (1887–1986). It was there that she established her home for over thirty years, with her main dwelling being an old adobe house, which she modernised with large windows and a flowing interior plan.

O'Keeffe grew up on a farm in Wisconsin. After studying art in Chicago and New York, she began working as an art teacher in Texas. Her experimentations in abstract art caught the attention of art dealer and photographer Alfred Stieglitz. He eventually became her husband and she moved to New York City, painting bold skyscrapers and flowers from the mid-1920s.

In the summer of 1929, O'Keeffe made the first of many trips to northern New Mexico. From 1934, she began staying at the scenic Ghost Ranch, in the same isolated traditional cottage surrounded by the undulating red and grey hills and the flat-topped Pedernal mountain, which she painted many times. After returning one summer to find it occupied, in 1940 she insisted on buying it as a summer house.

Too cold to stay there in winter, in 1945, she bought a single-storey house in nearby Abiquiú, which was built using the local adobe technique of baked clay and straw bricks, with a flat roof and softly curved corners. Partly dating back to the mid-18th century, it had been expanded in the 19th century in the Indigenous Pueblo style. O'Keeffe began a three-year renovation, working with her friend Maria Chabot, a rancher and advocate for Native American arts. They communicated via letters when she had to return to New York after her husband's death in 1946.

The walls were opened up with huge picture windows and skylights brought in more natural light from above. In the living room, a fireplace and display niches for collections of stones and bones were sculpted into the sand-coloured stucco walls, on which hung a pair of antlers attached to a skull. An old carriage house was rebuilt for her painting studio and bedroom.

Modern furniture included bent plywood chairs by Charles and Ray Eames and a lantern by Isamu Noguchi (see entry 31). Outside she planted a garden of native flowers and vegetables, and nature increasingly influenced her work, from landscapes to the clouds and sky. Today the Georgia O'Keeffe Museum owns both houses – the Abiquiú one, designated as a National Historic Landmark in 1998, is open to visitors, reflecting the artist's 1984 domestic arrangement.

ABOVE
The modernised Pueblo style house.

43

Donald Judd

New York City / Marfa, Texas, US

Art, furniture, architecture and living all became tools for the artist's concept of 'permanent installation', developed from the late 1960s.

For American artist Donald Judd (1928–1994) sculpture was inseparable from the space that surrounded it, as outlined in his 1980s theory of 'permanent installation' that united art, architecture and living. He expressed this total spatial concept at 101 Spring Street in New York and in Marfa, Texas, where he inhabited a series of buildings.

Judd was born in Missouri and served in the US Army 1946–47. On his return, he studied philosophy and art history at Columbia University, then painting at the Art Students League. After working as an art critic and painter, he started making boxy Minimalist sculptures resembling shelves and ladders in metal, Plexiglas and plywood.

In 1968, he purchased a five-storey cast-iron building that dated back to 1870, located in the former industrial neighbourhood of SoHo in New York City. He renovated it and designated functions for each floor, retaining the large open spaces for exhibiting art by friends such as Dan Flavin, Claes Oldenburg and John Chamberlain. He was one of the first artists to move into this Cast Iron District, and campaigned for its preservation, co-founding the 'Artists Against the Expressway' group with his wife Julie Finch.

He continued to explore architectural preservation when he expanded his 'permanent installation' idea to the town of Marfa, Texas. In the 1970s he bought two former aircraft hangars as a library and studio. He eventually bought a whole 'block', including an adobe house, a former grocery store, and a bank, barbershop and record store, renovating and dedicating each with a new function. He then founded the Chinati Foundation in Marfa in 1986 to exhibit large-scale installations.

The Marfa buildings were precisely furnished with his own plywood and metal designs, as well as Modern pieces by the likes of Alvar Aalto, Josef Albers, Ludwig Mies van der Rohe, Gerrit Rietveld and Theo van Doesburg. He installed long worktables and shelving for prototypes, material samples and architectural models.

ABOVE
The Marfa art studio, a former Safeway grocery store converted in 1990.

The Marfa buildings were precisely furnished with Judd's own plywood and metal designs.

After his death, the Judd Foundation, which he had made plans for from 1977, was established to preserve his living and working spaces as 'permanent installations', exactly as he intended. An architectural restoration of 101 Spring Street, initiated by Judd in the 1990s, was completed by the foundation in 2013, after which it opened to the public. Both this building and his 11 Marfa buildings are listed on the National Register of Historic Places.

ABOVE
The south library in Marfa.

44

Ruth Asawa

San Francisco, US

The domestic sphere became a modern universe for Asawa, who seamlessly blended art making with motherhood, education and advocacy.

The organic looped-wire sculptures of Japanese American artist Ruth Asawa (1926–2013) hung in constellations from the eaves of her early 20th-century Arts & Craft style home in San Francisco. She worked from a concrete-floored workshop downstairs designed by her husband, Modernist architect Albert Lanier, yet there were no boundaries between art and family life.

Born to Japanese immigrant parents, Asawa grew up in California with her six siblings, working on the family farm. After Japan entered World War II, in 1942 she was unjustly incarcerated aged 16 at a prison camp alongside 120,000 other people of Japanese descent. There, she learned to draw from three detained Walt Disney animators, which inspired her decision to become an art teacher. Prohibited from taking this pathway due to lingering anti-Japanese discrimination, she enrolled at the experimental Black Mountain College in North Carolina.

There, she studied under modern dancer Merce Cunningham, architect Buckminster Fuller and artist Josef Albers (an émigré from the Bauhaus school). On a trip to Mexico, she learned how to loop wire baskets, then developed the technique to make copper, brass and steel wire sculptures.

After working and living in San Francisco from the late 1940s, Asawa, Lanier and their six children moved into a cedar-shingled house in Noe Valley in 1960. Asawa carved the patterned redwood front doors in collaboration with her children, while inside, a sweeping staircase leads up to the rustic redwood-panelled living floor and down to the workshop where Asawa sculpted with plaster and wood, and soldered wire. The kitchen table was another workspace where she made plaster casts of visitors' faces and vegetables were drawn by the children before they were cooked for dinner.

Asawa extended this energy for art and children into the community as an advocate for arts education in public schools. She co-founded the Alvarado School Arts Workshop in 1968 and was instrumental in establishing a public arts high school in 1982, renamed the Ruth Asawa San Francisco School of the Arts in 2010.

ABOVE
The living room hung with sculptures.

45

Gordon Onslow Ford

California, US

A wooden 'ark' with a wave-shaped roof was a peaceful haven for a nature-loving Surrealist artist and his partner, a writer.

Surrealist artist Gordon Onslow Ford (1912–2003) was born in England, yet would build his house and studio near Inverness on the scenic Point Reyes peninsula in California. In harmony with nature, his timber 'ark' with a wave-shaped roof, built in 1958, placed him amid the mystical natural environment that inspired his paintings, which explored the cosmos through a language of curves, dots and lines.

Onslow Ford didn't study art, yet his grandfather was a sculptor and his uncle taught him painting. While serving in the navy in the 1930s he met artists Fernand Léger, André Lhôte and Roberto Matta in Paris; as soon as he could in 1939, he joined the Parisian Surrealist group, alongside a younger cohort including Yves Tanguy and Wolfgang Paalen. He developed his own technique, 'coulage', anticipating the 'action' painting of the Abstract Expressionists.

After being called to serve in World War II he returned to Britain, then in 1941 he travelled to New York, where his lectures attracted Jackson Pollock, Arshile Gorky and Mark Rothko. He soon left the city to remote Mexico with his wife, writer Jacqueline Johnson, where the landscape inspired his increasing pointillism and luminosity. In the late 1940s, they moved to San Francisco and Onslow Ford formed the Dynaton movement with Paalen and Matta.

In 1957, the couple bought 400 acres of pine forest north of San Francisco, carefully choosing a site for their house just below a ridge line for shelter and to preserve the view. They turned to an architect friend – Charles Warren Callister, who trained in Beaux Arts architecture, yet was informed by Frank Lloyd Wright and the Bay Area wood joinery tradition. The design process was collaborative; Johnson had previously worked with Modern architect Richard Neutra to build her former house in Los Altos in 1939.

The single-storey house has a curved- timber trussed roof beneath which flowed a bright, generous living space combining dining, bedroom and studio, flanked by a long galley for the entry and services. The roof rises to open up views through the

OPPOSITE
The house was carefully positioned in the landscape.

The house has a curved-timber trussed roof beneath which flowed a bright, generous living space decorated with art by friends and pre-Columbian sculptures.

south-facing wall of windows, shaded by the overhanging roof.

The grey-tinted wood-panel interior was decorated with art by friends Matta, Paalen, Ruth Asawa (see entry 44) and Lee Mullican; pre-Columbian sculptures from Mexico; and furniture made by musician Harry Partch and sculptor J B Blunk.

The latter had helped them build the house, and to thank him, the couple gave him some land on which to build his own house in 1959.

In 1998, Onslow Ford established the Lucid Art Foundation alongside Robert Anthoine and Fariba Bogzaran. After the couple's deaths, artist Bogzaran preserved and protected the house and studio, and later formed an artists and poets' residency there.

OPPOSITE
The living space with a large painting by Gordon Onslow Ford.

46

Frank Perry | Arthur Erickson

Vancouver, Canada

Japanese design meets West Coast Modernism at this dynamic wooden house in a forest in West Vancouver.

Canadian architect Arthur Erickson (1924–2009) designed a home for local artist Frank Perry (1923–2006) between 1961 and 1963. Located in West Vancouver in a forest near the North Shore Mountains, the house, studio and gallery was inspired by Japanese architecture and built of locally sourced fir and teak wood. Every room was connected to nature and the architecture created a dynamic spatial experience inside.

Partly pitched and partly flat, the roof is carved with openings, from skylights and clerestory windows to walls of glazing, creating an origami-like geometry of light and space. Moving through the house there is a sense of compression and expansion, with stepped levels between living spaces that lead down to a small office den.

Crafted surfaces add another layer to the atmosphere. The flooring is made of Japanese ceramic and mother-of-pearl tiles; the walls are lined with teak panelling. The cosy living room has a pine-slatted ceiling and wood-burning fireplace, while the main bedroom opens up to its own sunken courtyard garden. Perry's friend, Bill Reid, an artist of matrilineal descent of the Haida Nation, designed some of the home's wooden doors.

Perry, after serving overseas during World War II as part of the Royal Canadian Engineers, studied in British Columbia and then at art school in London until 1955. He worked as a teacher in Vancouver, while exhibiting his nature-informed abstract sculptures in Europe and Canada, including at the Vancouver Art Gallery. His 1960s bronze abstract public artwork can be seen outside Vancouver's Queen Elizabeth Theatre.

In designing the house, architect Erickson was informed by American architect Frank Lloyd Wright, known for how he integrated architecture into nature, yet also by Le Corbusier, in his functional approach to the open floorplan and daylight-infused spaces.

After World War II, Vancouver-born Erickson studied architecture at McGill University in Montreal and travelled widely to Cairo, Athens, Italy and Japan. On his return, he designed a series of houses in West Vancouver including Frank Perry's,

OPPOSITE
The bedroom.

The roof is carved with openings, from skylights and clerestory windows to walls of glazing, creating an origami-like geometry of light and space.

as well as houses for two other artists in collaboration with architect Geoffrey Massey.

These two houses were similarly dynamic wooden constructions, yet at a much larger scale and both situated on rocky land overlooking the sea: one for artist Ruth Killam in 1955 (who ended up marrying Massey); and the Smith Residence in 1964, conceived as a square spiral. The Perry House has been preserved by its private owner as an example of Erickson's environmentally sensitive and dynamic Modernism.

ABOVE
The house in the forest with its platform-like terrace.

47

Frida Kahlo and Diego Rivera | Juan O'Gorman

Mexico City, Mexico

The artist couple shared a colourful Early Modern house and studio complex designed by a like-minded architect and set within a cactus garden.

Mexican artist Frida Kahlo (1907–1954) – known for her candid, vibrant and introspective self-portraits – grew up in the leafy Coyoacán neighbourhood of Mexico City in the Casa Azul, a house built by her father in 1904. She also lived with her partner, the Mexican muralist Diego Rivera (1886–1957), in a Modernist house and studio complex designed by Mexican architect Juan O'Gorman (1905–1982) from 1929 to 1931, which is recognised as an early example of Modernism in Mexico.

Kahlo grew up in post-revolution Mexico City, a period of national pride and cultural reinvention, though her life was defined by illness: she had polio as a child and a traumatic bus accident as a teenager left her with chronic pain. Her family home, Casa Azul, became her universe, where she painted symbolic portraits with modern clarity informed by pre-Hispanic aesthetics.

She met Rivera (20 years her senior) around 1922, when he was painting a mural at her school; they married in 1929. Rivera had studied traditional painting and sculpting from a young age and travelled extensively in Europe, studying Renaissance frescoes. His modern style was informed by Picasso and Seurat as well as his own political activism: he was a member of the Mexican Communist Party in 1922 and he founded the Revolutionary Union of Technical Workers, Painters and Sculptors. He boldly depicted industrial and agricultural workers in murals across Mexico and the US.

OPPOSITE
Frida Kahlo's blue house and studio raised on pilotis.

Rivera's red-and-white house-studio was connected by a rooftop bridge to Kahlo's blue house-studio.

O'Gorman, who had studied architecture in Mexico City, was a fellow communist, respected for his contributions to Functionalist working-class housing and public schools. His design for the house and studio for Kahlo and Rivera was inspired by Le Corbusier's 1922 studio-house for artist Amédée Ozenfant in Paris (see entry 7), yet was distinctly Mexican with traditional colours, curved sculptural staircases and a cactus garden.

The site consists of two house-studios, and a photographic laboratory for Kahlo's father, Guillermo. Rivera's red-and-white concrete house-studio is partly raised on pilotis with a sawtooth roof and grids of windows. A rooftop bridge connected it to Kahlo's blue house-studio. The couple lived and worked there together for a few years, until Kahlo moved back to Casa Azul.

After Rivera's death, the structures were modified, yet later sold to the National Institute of Fine Arts, and opened to the public as a museum in 1986. A 1990s restoration returned its original design and it was designated a National Landmark. Casa Azul, extended by O'Gorman in the 1940s, opened in 1958 as a house museum that tells the story of Kahlo's life.

ABOVE AND OPPOSITE
Spiralling concrete staircases designed by architect Juan O'Gorman.

48

Tomie Ohtake | Ruy Ohtake

São Paulo, Brazil

Colourful, curvy concrete architecture reflected the abstract aesthetic of the artist and the organic nature of Brazilian Modernism.

The house and studio of Japanese Brazilian artist Tomie Ohtake (1913–2015) was designed by her son, architect Ruy Ohtake (1938–2021) and built in São Paulo in 1970. Just like her colourful, geometric works, which spanned from painting to sculpture and public art, the architecture embraces both geometric and free-flowing volumes.

From the shady entrance in the blue-painted facade, the exposed concrete interior expands and compresses with angles, shadows and blocks of primary colours. Integrated furniture forms a Brutalist landscape for seating, books, objects and artworks, while enclosed volumes hide bedrooms and bathrooms. The large double-height studio has a huge roof-light and sliding glass doors open up to the courtyard garden and pool.

Kyoto-born artist Ohtake had been visiting one of her brothers in Brazil in the mid-1930s when the increasing military tensions at home prevented her return. She settled in Brazil in 1936, where she married and had two children. She began painting and, encouraged by artist Keiya Sugano, joined the Seibi group of Japanese artists in Brazil.

From the 1950s she embraced abstraction, using magazine collages as prototypes for paintings and prints. Moving into the new studio expanded the scale of her work to larger canvases and monumental public sculptures from the late 1980s in iron, concrete, steel and glass. In designing the space, Ruy Ohtake was inspired by his mother's art as well as earlier Brazilian Modernist architects such as Oscar Niemeyer. He then went on to design other poetically geometric houses in the same spirit.

The house evolved with an extension after 16 years, adding a new dining room and archive, and it became a social meeting place for friends, family, artists, curators and journalists. Tomie lived and worked there until the age of 101, and the house remains a tribute to her legacy in São Paulo, where the Tomie Ohtake Institute is established.

ABOVE
The curved concrete roof shades an outdoor seating area.

OVERLEAF
The interior layered with bold colours, plants and integrated furniture.

EM OBRAS: HISTORIA DO VAZIO EM BELO HORIZONTE
Museums

49

Oswaldo Guayasamín | Gustavo Guayasamín

Quito, Ecuador

This lively Modernist hacienda housed a music hall, painting studio, library and museum, as well as the symbolic, artist-designed Chapel of Man.

Ecuadorian artist Oswaldo Guayasamín (1919–1999) sketched a Modernist hacienda-style home and studio complex in the 1970s, which was built by his architect brother Gustavo Guayasamín (1925-2007). Located in Quito's Bellavista neighbourhood on Guangüiltagua Hill, the architecture distilled regional Hispanic and Andean design elements into a functionalist building of block-like volumes.

Quito-born Guayasamín studied art in the 1930s and travelled to the US in 1942, where he admired art by El Greco and Goya in museums. He apprenticed with muralist José Clemente Orozco in Mexico, then developed his own style blending Cubism and Abstract Expressionism informed by social history, Ecuadorean folk art, and his own political views as a communist.

His house and studio grew into a cultural destination for the community with a large hall for dining and musical concerts beyond the arched cloister. There was one bedroom, a library, painting studio and wine cellar in the main house, and over time guest houses and the pool were added.

Around 1985, Guayasamín began designing the Capilla del Hombre (Chapel of Man), a square stone structure with a metal, cone-shaped roof that paid homage to Latin American history. Set over two levels with an interior of black volcanic Laja stone floor and native Chanul wood, it was carefully planned around the path of the sun during solstices and equinoxes. Construction began in 1996 and it was inaugurated in 2002.

Founded by the artist in 1976, the Guayasamín Foundation opened the house and studio as a museum in 2012, which houses the largest collection of his work, as well as his collections of pre-Columbian ceramics, bone and metal artefacts; religious art; and art of the Escuela Quiteña (Quito School). Guayasamín is buried alongside his friend, Ecuadorian writer and poet Jorge Enrique Adoum, under a pine tree near the house.

OPPOSITE
The white facade of the main house.

50 Edgardo Giménez

Buenos Aires, Argentina

Pop Art meets Postmodernism at the 1970s houses of the artist who designed graphic posters and film scenography.

With no formal training in architecture, Argentine artist and designer Edgardo Giménez (b. 1942) designed a series of playful houses with integrated interiors from the early 1970s. His iterative process resulted in a style that riffs between Radical design, Postmodern architecture and Pop Art.

Giménez began his artistic life drawing graphics for an advertising company in Santa Fe, Argentina, where he was born. He had been drawn to Hollywood and Disney movies from a young age, and went on to design theatre posters and later scenography for films.

The artist joined the Buenos Aires avant-garde Pop-art scene of the 1960s, alongside artists Marta Minujín, Juan Stoppani and designer Delia Cancela. He travelled to New York City in 1967, seeing art by Andy Warhol and Roy Lichtenstein, which contributed to the evolution of his design vision of interiors, furniture and clothes, which anticipated the Radical design of the Memphis movement (see entry 12) in Italy.

The Buenos Aires scene centred around the influential Di Tella Institute (Institut Torcuato di Tella), which was forced to close in 1970 by the military dictatorship that governed Argentina from 1966–73. Its founders Jorge Romero Brest and Martita Bontempi then created the 'Out of the Box Center for Consuming Art' (Fuera de Caja Centro de Arte para Consumir), a collective for artist-designed objects for which Giménez created a series of extroverted items from towers to kittens in materials from porcelain to crystal.

After this collaboration, Brest and Bontempi commissioned Giménez to design the interior of their Buenos Aires house (1969–70), which he lined with mirrors and chrome-plated fly screens on the ceilings. Happy with the eccentric result, they asked him to design them a weekend retreat in City Bell: equally bold, the Casa Azul (1971–72) was bright blue with rainbows on its arched facades.

In 1979, the house was exhibited as part of MoMA's 'Transformations in Modern Architecture' exhibition of bizarre designs, alongside Disneyland in Orlando and Le Corbusier's vaulted Maisons Jaoul. Giménez designed further houses,

OPPOSITE
Casa Neptuna.

including the yellow temple-like Casa Amarilla (1979–81) in Punta Indio, and the retrofuturistic aluminium interior of Discotec Soho club (1987) in Buenos Aires.

He channelled his design approach into working as art director of the Teatro San Martín in the early 1980s, and directed visual communications for the culture department of the Buenos Aires City Government from 2000 to 2006. In 2021, he designed the bright green Casa Neptuna in José Ignacio, Uruguay, for art collector Amalia Amoedo: a live-work house for two artists in residence with a technicoloured roof of shapes.

LEFT
Casa Amarilla.

RIGHT
Interior of the Casa de las Columnas Doradas.

The 20th-Century Artist's House Museum

What is the magic of the modern artist's house museum – and what does it take to keep them alive?

It was during the Renaissance period in Europe from around the 15th century that artists first started signing their names on works, as the artist and artisan slowly began separating in recognition of unique individual talent. Italian writer Giorgio Vasari's book *Lives of the Artists*, published in 1550, recounted the stories of Leonardo da Vinci, Michelangelo and Raphael among others, tracing their personal journeys and artistic process. There was intrigue in the life of the artist.

The social status of artists was slowly shifting. Late-18th-century Neoclassical and Romantic painters captivated audiences as translators of both reason and the mysteries of life, while the 19th century saw artists becoming mirrors and critics of social and political life, emerging onto the public stage. In the 20th century, the avant-garde artist evolved as a radical free-thinker, their identities captured in evocative self-portraiture and magnified by the growth of modern media (photography, film, magazines, interviews) that eventually created the consumable 'celebrity'.

Perhaps even more personal than the artworks they share and project out into the world, the artist's house is an intimate manifestation of their identity. In the 21st century, artists' house museums have become sacred pilgrimages for art lovers to immerse within the aura of an artist. They are not confined to a straightforward typology – they exist in many formats from domestic shrines preserved in their entirety with sacred paint splatters, to artist's theme parks evolved with galleries, cafes, shops and research centres.

The art of the artist's house museum is certainly not an easy one – after the death of the artist, homes and studios transfer into the hands of family members, estates and national museum collections to be preserved and managed. Many don't survive, yet remain with us in photos, letters and books. The great task of opening them up to the public requires resources and ambition alike: yet the result is moving and inspiring to us all, allowing us to absorb the artist's memories, desires and dreams.

Legacy building

The establishment of an artist's house museum is sure to have an impact on their legacy – and how successfully it lives on. The living spaces of Mexican artist Frida Kahlo have inspired three house museums in Mexico City: the Casa Azul, her family home; the house-studio she shared with her muralist husband Diego Rivera (see entry 47), opened 1986; and the Casa Roja, at a family house where she spent time, opened 2025.

From the 1980s the price of Kahlo's work at auction soared into the millions. (1) It was the beginning of 'Fridamania': she gained a cult following globally, her portrait replicated on fridge magnets, coasters and T-shirts. Her image is closely tied to the preservation of Casa Azul: in 2004, after 50 years, her dressing room was 'unsealed', revealing her most intimate possessions of traditional Tehuana dresses, painted medical corsets, lipsticks and eyebrow pencils.

Hilda Trujillo, former director of the Museo Frida Kahlo, recalled: 'I felt like an intruder, for what right do I have to be there with Frida's things? At times I thought I wasn't entitled to do this, that no-one was.' (2) Is the powerful dimension of privacy and its disturbance essential to creating the 'aura' of an artist's house museum?

Modern philosophers Hannah Arendt and Walter Benjamin explored the heightened sanctity of private space in the 20th century, as a product of the increasing social demands of public space in all areas from work, to travel and entertainment. In this context, Arendt believed we all need a 'hiding place' where we can embrace the full spectrum of being human, the darkness and the light. (3)

When it is exposed, does an artist's house then become a stage? Kahlo exposed her innermost thoughts in life through her paintings, no matter how painful. Opening her house after her death, even revealing her most personal sanctum, seems like an extension of her artistic practice – her ability to share her vulnerability in life remains after her death in the authentic aura of her house.

Ready-made house museum

Once an artist dies, they relinquish control of their image to some extent, relying on later generations to package it up for public consumption. Minimalist sculptor Donald Judd was an artist who thought carefully about this during his lifetime. His concept of 'permanent installation' outlined that the exact placement of art within architecture – including that within his own homes in New York and Marfa (see entry 43) – was fundamental to its understanding, and therefore must be preserved in place.

In 1977 he designed a blueprint for a foundation to preserve his 'permanent installations' after his death. (4) So if he lived and worked inside spaces that he knew would be preserved after his death: did he already live inside his own house museum? The foundation was established in 1994 after his death by his children, Flavin and Rainer, and they followed his plan with meticulous care and impressive commitment.

Today, a visit to Judd's New York home at 101 Spring Street is a pilgrimage. It is a quiet, intimate, guided experience with a small group and no photography or videos are allowed,

Georgia O'Keeffe at home in 1971

Artists' house museums have become sacred pilgrimages for art lovers to immerse within the aura of an artist.

heightening the sacred quality of visiting in person. The foundation publishes books, catalogues, online texts and information, forming an incredible, accessible archive on the artist – all stylistically designed, an exemplary 'packaging' that with every decision captures far more than a space, rather embodying the whole philosophy of Judd.

Sometimes the artist isn't really the writer of their own 'house museum' and its story is about how we interpret it today as readers.

Houses with lives of their own

In other cases, houses have evolved far beyond what an artist ever could have imagined – into new kinds of contemporary curated, reframed and recontextualised expressions. In Marrakech, Jacques Majorelle's house, studio and botanic garden (see entry 34) are now the site of the Yves Saint Laurent Museum, a building by French architects Studio KO and opened in 2017. Its content and design are dedicated to the second-generation 'guardians' (fashion designer Yves Saint Laurent and his partner Pierre Bergé) of the original 'artist's house', resulting in a layered creation: the story that began in 1923, over a hundred years ago, continues to be written.

Sometimes the artist isn't really the writer of their own 'house museum' and its story is about how we interpret and apply meaning to it today as readers, relative to the development of culture. The artist therefore might not see their house as meaningful, aesthetic or worthy of museum status – until someone enters after their death to recognise that meaning.

In Reykjavik, the Sigurjón Ólafsson Museum emerged from the initiative of the artist's widow Inga Birgitta Spur after his death; she commissioned the son of the original Modernist architect to redesign the workshop and part of the house into a gallery, archive and cafe. Hlíf Sigurjonsdottir, daughter of Ólafsson and Spur, is fiercely passionate for the recognition of Spur as integral to both artist and museum, and for her the museum is about preserving her mother's legacy too.

Sigurjonsdottir's son, Jón Hlífarson Geirfinnsson, with Simone Hart, created a short film about Spur: an intimate portrait of her character, set partly within the 'artist's house', which during the artist's life was of no interest to him: he lived to work. Domestic life inside the house with four children was conducted on a shoe-string, yet Spur brought warmth with her intelligence and resourcefulness. The film captures the hypnotic blue sea horizon framed within a picture window, the soft light illuminating sculptures, books and the yellow tones of the pine-wood panels. For voyeurs into this world it is magical, though for Sigurjonsdottir, the reality of her childhood memories are ever-present. (5)

Reconstructions

To some extent, we exoticise the 'artist's house'. So much so, that we have even placed them inside museums like artefacts – to view and not touch. At Hannover's Sprengel Museum, a 1980s reconstruction of Kurt Schwitters' site-specific house interior, the 'Merzbau' (see entry 14) is on display: the 16-year project inside a Hannover house was destroyed in 1943 during World War II. At the Triennale di Milano, the original 1965 interior of Casa Lana designed by Ettore Sottsass (see entry 12) for his friend lithographer and printer Giovanni Lana was reconstructed in 2022.

'It is as if Casa Lana was frozen in time, precisely as the architect designed it. This allows us to present a project in its totality, integrity and strength,' remarked curator Marco Sammicheli upon its opening. (6) What can we learn from the preservation of their exact dimensions and atmospheres? Can they teach us how to live better?

In the case of Ena de Silva's house (see entry 35) in Sri Lanka, designed by Tropical Modernist Geoffrey Bawa in the 1960s, to save it from demolition it was painstakingly disassembled in Colombo in 2009 and reconstructed – 'stone by stone' – by a team of architects, archaeologists and engineers at Bawa's Lunuganga Estate in Bentota, south of Colombo, between 2012 and 2016. (7) Rather than a museum, it is now part of a hotel that fully honours its design, history and identity, while incorporating three guest rooms (with the contemporary comforts of a king-sized bed and minibar).

Sleepovers

So while we might visit a museum to admire and reflect on the design and concept of an artist's house, we might also stay overnight inside one for a more intimate experience, of sleeping, dreaming, waking up, reading, writing, absorbing nature and light – reliving the modern life of the artist for yourself. Perhaps it's the closest way to get inside an artist's head and to see life through their eyes and perspective.

You can also stay at Arakawa and Gins' Mitaka Lofts (see entry 39) in Tokyo for a mind-bending conceptual experience that may extend your life through its activating interior – or on the Bauhaus campus in Dessau in the student accommodation (not in the Masters' Houses, see entry 13), where Functionalist rooms with original furniture are full of light and optimism.

Greek architect Dionisis Sotovikis, who lives in the former studio-house of Ioanna Veropoulou-Spiteri and Tonis Spiteris (see entry 27), does not live in a house museum. It is a social meeting place for conversations and ideas, a place he spent years researching and restoring, and continues to curate exhibitions about, open up for tours, and invite students and curious visitors inside for coffee. It inspires his own work as an architect everyday: 'You have to respect what came before you to be able to build something for the future,' he says. (8)

What was evident when we started and now where we end up, is that 20th-century artist's house museums are places that mix inspiration, education and aspiration with a powerful human bond, connected to both everyday life and dreaming. In a new century where much of the optimism and perspective of the Modernists has been lost, the ability to step back in time into an artist's house certainly holds some nostalgia and romanticism.

Artist's house museums are far more than a weekend day trip and a cultural experience, they're an antidote, a lesson and perhaps even a warning of what's at stake in this century: a space of one's own to externalise our inner thoughts; a place to dream outside the bounds of convention; a place to defy the binaries imposed on us by society and reconnect with things that we treasure; and a place to feel at home in ourselves, so when we step outside, we can be radical and brave.

References

Introduction

1. Pallasmaa, J. (2013) 'Towards a Neuroscience of Architecture: Embodied Mind and Imagination', Tidwell, P (ed). *Architecture and Neuroscience*. Tapio Wirkkala – Rut Bryk Foundation. p9.
2. Klein, S. (2021) *The See-Through House: My Father in Full Colour*. Vintage. p5.
3. Hess, A. (1985) 'Charles Warren Callister's Onslow-Ford House', *Fine Homebuilding*, June/July No. 27. p27.

Modern Art Meets the Modern House

1. Droste, M. (2019) *Bauhaus 1919-1933*. Taschen. p182.
2. Cohen, J L. (2013) *Le Corbusier, An Atlas of Modern Landscapes*. Thames & Hudson. pp27–28.
3. Davies, C. (2017) *A New History of Modern Architecture*. Laurence King Publishing.
4. Droste, M. (2019) Bauhaus 1919–1933. Taschen. p359.
5. Rudofsky, B. (1964) *Architecture without architects, an introduction to nonpedigreed architecture*. The Museum of Modern Art, Doubleday. Available at: moma.org/documents/moma_catalogue_3459_300062280.pdf (Accessed: 20 July 2025).
6. Emilio A. (ed). (1972) Italy: the new domestic landscape achievements and problems of Italian design. Museum of Modern Art, New York Graphic Society. Available at: assets.moma.org/documents/moma_catalogue_1783_300062429.pdf (Accessed: 20 July 2025).

The House in Modern Art

1. Nadeau, M. (1989) *The History of Surrealism*. Harvard University Press. p241.
2. Hessel, K. (2022) *The Story of Art Without Men*. Hutchinson Heinemann. p120.
3. Ibid, p122.
4. Ibid, p169.

5. Kessas, S. (2024) Podcast. Episode 4: 'The influence of the workshop house'. Bozar, Palais des Beaux-arts de Bruxelles.
6. Cummings, L. (2022) 'Léon Wuidar review – exquisite blueprints for imagined places', the *Guardian*. Available at: theguardian.com/artanddesign/2022/sep/04/leon-wuidar-white-cube-masons-yard-london-review-exquisite-blueprints-for-imagined-places (Accessed 20 August 2025).
7. Madsen, A K and Oehler, S K. (2024) 'Skyscraper Living: Georgia O'Keeffe and the Shelton Hotel', Art Institute Chicago. Available at: artic.edu/articles/1126/skyscraper-living-georgia-o-keeffe-and-the-shelton-hotel (Accessed 20 August 2025).
8. Shinohara, K. (1962) 'A house is a work of art', *Shinkenchiku*, vol.37, No1.
9. Simmons, L. (No date) Museum of Modern Art audio transcription (moma.org/artists/7015-laurie-simmons#fn:1) (Accessed 25 August 2025).

The 20th-Century Artist's House Museum

1. Trebay, G. (2015) 'Frida Kahlo is Having a Moment', *New York Times*. Available at: nytimes.com/2015/05/10/style/frida-kahlo-is-having-a-moment.html (Accessed 1 September 2025).
2. Anon. (2024) 'Unlocking Frida Kahlo's wardrobe', Victoria and Albert Museum. vam.ac.uk/articles/unlocking-frida-kahlos-wardrobe (Accessed 1 September 2025).
3. Arendt, H. (1998) *The Human Condition*. University of Chicago Press.
4. Judd, D. (1977) 'Donald Judd Writings', Donald Judd Foundation. Available at: juddfoundation.org/donald-judd/writing (Accessed 5 September 2025).
5. Sigurjonsdottir, H. (2025) Telephone interview with Hlíf Sigurjonsdottir, 3 October 2025.
6. Didero, M C. (2022) 'Compact apartment by Ettore Sottsass reveals pioneering design approach', *Wallpaper**. Available at: (wallpaper.com/design/ettore-sottsass-casa-lana-triennale-milan) (Accessed 5 September 2025).
7. Anon. (No date). 'No.05 Lunuganga', Geoffrey Bawa Trust. https://geoffreybawa.com/number-05 (Accessed 1 September 2025).
8. Sotovikis, D. (2025) Telephone interview Dionisis Sotovikis, 1 October 2025.

Acknowledgements

Thank you to all artists' estates, foundations and family members for inspiring conversations, generous collaboration and openness to sharing your knowledge and insights. It's been an honour learning about the lives of these 20th century artists and architects through you. Thank you for sharing these houses and preserving them for future generations.

Thank you to the photographers who have brought this book to life through their lenses: each photo tells its own story of a house through your own artistic perspectives. Thank you to Adiva Lawrence, Tom Howells and Sam Thorne, writers and thinkers who I admire, for your thoughts on the development of the essays.

Thank you to my parents for taking me to the houses of Monet and Gabriele Münter as a child, and for always opening up art books to show me the colours and shapes of Modern Art from a young age.

Thank you to Rebecca Armstrong at Batsford for inviting me to join this thought-provoking journey into exploring the connections between domesticity and creativity in the 20th century.

About the Author

Harriet Thorpe is a British journalist and author based in London. She studied History of Art at SOAS and Journalism at City University in London. Interested in art, architecture and heritage of the 20th century period, she writes for leading design magazines including *Wallpaper** and *The World of Interiors*. She has contributed words to books on topics from Tropical Modernism to legends of Italian design, houses on the Côte d'Azur and environmentally-conscious urban buildings and parks.

ABOVE AND LEFT
The author with her sister, and her mother, both at Monet's house in Giverny in the 1990s.

Picture Credits

Cover
Front: Frank Perry's house by the white space co.
Back: Top left: César Manrique, Harriet Thorpe
Middle top: Casa Lana by Ettore Sottsass, Harriet Thorpe
Top right: Floris Jespers's house, LUCID
Middle right: Casa de las Columnas Doradas, Edgardo Giménez
Bottom right: Joan Miro's house, Collection: Fundació Pilar i Joan Miró a Mallorca

2: © Harriet Thorpe; 6: photo courtesy of the Bernat Klein Foundation; 9: Ruth Asawa and her children Xavier, Aiko, Adam, Addie Laurie, and Paul Lanier working with Baker's Clay in the kitchen of their Noe Valley home, San Francisco, CA, c. 1964-65. Photo by Gordon Peters. Artwork © 2026 Ruth Asawa Lanier, Inc., Courtesy David Zwirner; 12: © Adam Štěch; 14–15: © Adam Štěch; 17: © Romain Laprade; 18: © Romain Laprade; 20: © Galerie Natalie Seroussi; 22–23: © Galerie Natalie Seroussi; 24: © Jean-Michel Bale; 27: © Mary Gaudin; 29: © François du Chatenet; 30: © Laurent Kruszyk, Île-de-France Region; 32–33: © Laurent Kruszyk, Île-de-France Region; 35: © Alamy / Hemis; 36: Alamy / B.O'Kane; 39: © Jean-Pierre Dalbéra, licensed under the Creative Commons Attribution 2.0 Generic license (https://creativecommons.org/licenses/by/2.0/deed.en); 41: © Adam Štěch; 42: © Alamy / imageBROKER.com; 44: © Alamy / Andia; 47: © M3Studio; 49: © Harriet Thorpe; 50–51: © Harriet Thorpe; 52: © Robert Rieger; 54: © Robert Rieger; 55: © Tillmann Franzen; 56: © © bpk | Sprengel Museum Hannover | Michael Herling | Aline Gwose; 59: © Jürg Zimmermann Zürich; 61: © Digital image Whitney Museum of American Art / Licensed by Scala; 69: © Alice Inggs, The World of Interiors, © Condé Nast; 70: © Collection: Fundació Pilar i Joan Miró a Mallorca © for the works by Joan Miró: Successió Miró, 2026 © Juan Gavilán; 72–73: Collection: Fundació Pilar i Joan Miró a Mallorca © for the works by Joan Miró: Successió Miró, 2026 © Juan Gavilán; 75: © Daniel Schaefer; 76: © Sayana Cairo www.sayanacairo.com; 79: © Sayana Cairo www.sayanacairo.com; 81: © pere prlpz, licensed under the Creative Commons Attribution-Share Alike 3.0 Unported licensed (https://creativecommons.org/licenses/by-sa/3.0/deed.en); 83: © Harriet Thorpe; 84: © Harriet Thorpe; 85: © Harriet Thorpe; 86–87: © Harriet Thorpe; 88: © Victor Robin; 91: © Piet-Albert Goethals; 92–93: © Piet-Albert Goethals; 94: © LUCID; 96: © LUCID; 97: © LUCID; 98: Barbara Hepworth © Bowness; 101: Barbara Hepworth © Bowness; 102 (above and below): © Taran Wilkhu; 104–105: © Taran Wilkhu; 106: © Taran Wilkhu; 107: © Taran Wilkhu; 109: © Architect Dionisis Sotovikis; 110: © Ivan Brodey; 112: © Ivan Brodey; 113: © Ivan Brodey; 115: © Geirfinnur Jónsson; 116–117: © Geirfinnur Jónsson; 119: Arakawa and Gins, Drawing for Container of Perceiving, 1984. Acrylic, watercolor, and pencil on paper; 42½ x 72 in. (108 x 182.9 cm). Photo by Nicholas Knight. © 2018 Reversible Destiny Foundation. Reproduced with permission of the Reversible Destiny Foundation; 124: Alamy / Enrico Salvadori; 127 © Takashi Yasumura; 128: © Takashi Homma; 131: © Takashi Homma; 133: Interior courtyard with rainwater oculus feeding a shallow basin once used to sustain small fish and other water creatures, New Culture Studios, Ibadan, Oyo State, Nigeria. © Fawaz Oyedeji, February 2024; 134–135: Exterior view from the open-air theatre section of New Culture Studios, Ibadan, Oyo State, Nigeria. © Fawaz Oyedeji, February 2024; 136: © Thomas Lannes; 139: © Geoffrey Bawa and Lunuganga Trusts; 140–141: © Geoffrey Bawa and Lunuganga Trusts; 142: © Nick Sissons; 144–145: © Paul Lovelace / Alamy; 147: © Michael Borowski; 148: © Stewards; 151: © 1997 Reversible Destiny Foundation. Reproduced with permission of the Reversible Destiny Foundation Courtesy of the Site of Reversible Destiny—Yoro Park; 152: © 1997 Reversible Destiny Foundation. Reproduced with permission of the Reversible Destiny Foundation Courtesy of the Site of Reversible Destiny—Yoro Park; 155: © Frelinghuysen Morris House & Studio, Lenox, Massachusetts. Used by permission. All rights reserved.; 156–157: © Frelinghuysen Morris House & Studio, Lenox, Massachusetts. Used by permission. All rights reserved.; 159: Exterior of the East Hampton, New York studio and home of Abstract Jaime Ardiles-Arce, Architectural Digest, © Condé Nast; 160: Dining room in the adobe house of artist Georgia O'Keeffe at Ghost Robert Reck, Architectural Digest, ©Condé Nast; 163: Breakfast room, with a table topped by a vase of yellow daisies, in Robert Reck, Architectural Digest, © Condé Nast; 165: © Judd Foundation; 166: © Judd Foundation; 169: Ruth Asawa in the living room of her Noe Valley home, San Francisco, CA, c. 1995.
Artwork © 2026 Ruth Asawa Lanier, Inc., Courtesy David Zwirner; 170: © Ekaterina Izmestieva; 173: © Ekaterina Izmestieva; 175: © the white space co.; 176–177: © the white space co.; 178: © Marina Denisova / Kintzing; 180: © Marina Denisova / Kintzing; 181: © Marina Denisova / Kintzing; 183: © Nelson Kon; 184–185: © Nelson Kon; 186: © Adam Štěch; 189: © Cortesía Fundación Ama Amoedo. Ph. Cristobal Palma.; 190: © Edgardo Giménez; 191: © Edgardo Giménez; 195: Alamy / Science History Images; 202 (left and right): Harriet Thorpe

Index

BATSFORD

Editorial Director Lauren Whybrow
Commissioning Editor Rebecca Armstrong
Art Director Eoghan O'Brien
Junior Designer Sanya Jain
Head of Production Morna McPherson
Production Controller Pete Rouse

Layout design by Kei Ishimaru

First published in the United Kingdom
in 2026 by
Batsford
43 Great Ormond Street
London
WC1N 3HZ

An imprint of B. T. Batsford Holdings Limited

ISBN 9781837330263

A CIP catalogue record for this book is available from the British Library.

10 9 8 7 6 5 4 3 2 1

Reproduction by Rival Colour Ltd, UK
Printed by Dream Colour, China

This book can be ordered direct from the publisher at www.batsfordbooks.com,
or try your local bookshop.

Distributed throughout the UK and Europe by Abrams & Chronicle Books, 1st Floor, 22–24 Ely Place, London EC1N 6TE and 57 rue Gaston Tessier, 75166 Paris, France

www.abramsandchronicle.co.uk
info@abramsandchronicle.co.uk

FSC www.fsc.org MIX Paper | Supporting responsible forestry FSC® C188448